Routledge Revivals

An Outline of Anglo-Saxon Grammar

First published in 1936, this book is intended to provide an outline of Anglo-Saxon grammar for beginners, focusing on well-selected, succinctly stated rules rather than giving a detailed survey. It focuses on the West-Saxon dialect as this is best suited to beginners due to its uniformity in phonology and inflection, the fact it forms the basis of Anglo-Saxon grammar, and its prominence in the extant literature. Extracts have been selected from this literature to provide a sufficient basis, via the study of the easier to grasp later form of the dialect, to prepare the reader for the more difficult early West-Saxon dialect and further chronological study of the texts.

An Outline of Anglo-Saxon Grammar

Published as an Appendix to "An Anglo-Saxon Reader"

James W. Bright

First published in 1936
by George Allen & Unwin

This edition first published in 2017 by Routledge
2 Park Square, Milton Park, Abingdon, Oxon, OX14 4RN
and by Routledge
711 Third Avenue, New York, NY 10017

Routledge is an imprint of the Taylor & Francis Group, an informa business

© 1936 James W. Bright

All rights reserved. No part of this book may be reprinted or reproduced or utilised in any form or by any electronic, mechanical, or other means, now known or hereafter invented, including photocopying and recording, or in any information storage or retrieval system, without permission in writing from the publishers.

Publisher's Note
The publisher has gone to great lengths to ensure the quality of this reprint but points out that some imperfections in the original copies may be apparent.

Disclaimer
The publisher has made every effort to trace copyright holders and welcomes correspondence from those they have been unable to contact.

A Library of Congress record exists under LC control number: 10033843

ISBN 13: 978-1-138-23707-0 (hbk)
ISBN 13: 978-1-315-30071-9 (ebk)
ISBN 13: 978-1-138-23711-7 (pbk)

AN OUTLINE OF
ANGLO-SAXON GRAMMAR
PUBLISHED AS AN APPENDIX TO
"AN ANGLO-SAXON READER"

by

JAMES W. BRIGHT, Ph.D.

Revised and Enlarged by
JAMES R. HULBERT, Ph.D.
*Professor of English
in the University of Chicago*

LONDON
GEORGE ALLEN & UNWIN LTD
MUSEUM STREET

FIRST PUBLISHED 1895
SECOND IMPRESSION . 1901
THIRD IMPRESSION . . 1906
FOURTH IMPRESSION . 1911
FIFTH IMPRESSION . . 1917
SIXTH IMPRESSION . . 1921
REVISED AND ENLARGED EDITION 1936

All rights reserved

PRINTED IN GREAT BRITAIN BY
KIMBLE & BRADFORD LONDON, W.I.

PREFATORY NOTE

In revising a book which has stood the test of extensive use for forty years, it is desirable to make as few changes as possible. Hence the alterations in this edition of Bright's *Reader* are limited to (1) such changes in the grammar as are necessary to bring it into accord with current views, (2) a few corrections in the texts, glossary, and outline of versification, (3) substitution for the last part of *The Phoenix* and all the Latin poem, of selections from Anglo-Saxon poetry, (4) addition of a glossary for these poems, and (5) insertion of a sketch of Anglo-Saxon literature. No attempt has been made to expand the outline of grammar, since experience has shown that Bright's well-selected, succinctly stated rules are better adapted to the needs of beginners than detailed surveys which delight a specialist in linguistics.

The added poems were chosen with the aim of providing at least the essential parts of some of the most famous pieces in Anglo-Saxon, and of illustrating as wide a range of forms as possible. *Deor's Lament*, *Widsith*, *Waldere*, *The Fight at Finnsburg* were not included because they are available in the best editions of *Beowulf*. The supplementary glossary follows the form of Bright's *Glossary* except that it does not give principal parts of verbs or "etymological hints" and rarely quotes the cited words.

Finally, since the sources of information available to most students on Anglo-Saxon literature are based on the scholarship of forty or fifty years ago, and since at the time when students are learning the elements of Anglo-Saxon grammar

PREFATORY NOTE

and reading texts they should have a knowledge of the relation of the selections to Anglo-Saxon literature as a whole, I have included a brief sketch of that subject. It is not documented and is merely such a running account as a lecturer might give in a classroom. It does not present original or individual views, but of course selection and emphasis must be to some extent personal.

For the corrections in texts, glossary, and outline of versification I am indebted to Professor B. C. Monroe of Cornell University.

J. R. HULBERT.

PREFACE.

THE first three of the following paragraphs are from the former Preface of this book.

In the choice of texts by which the student is to be introduced to the language and literature of Anglo-Saxon times, an editor is compelled, in view of the practical end, to suppress many considerations: there must be gradation that may contradict chronology, or dialectal relationship; there must be a degree of variety that may do violence to completeness. An adjustment in partial harmony with all reasonable requirements is as much as can be hoped for.

The West-Saxon dialect, though not exactly in the line of the subsequent development of the language, is yet best adapted to the conditions of the beginner, for it possesses sufficient uniformity in phonology and inflection, the gram-

PREFACE.

mars are based upon it, and it embraces most of the literature. The style and the character of the literature also determine the easiest introduction to be through the later form of this dialect. The following texts have been selected and arranged in accordance with these views. The first three extracts are intended to supply a sufficient basis for an elementary preparation that will fit the student to pass to the study of the Early West-Saxon dialect, and thereafter to read the literature in chronological order. Any slight admixture of dialectal forms will be easily understood by the use of Sievers' Grammar.

Orthographic variation (chiefly due to chronological differences in the texts) has made difficult a compact yet clear arrangement of the glossary; however, the variant forms in parentheses, the principal parts of the verbs, and the citations will be found, it is believed, to mitigate the somewhat sparing use of cross-references. The etymological hints conveyed either in the definitions or by the bracketed forms will suggest some of the fundamental principles of derivation, but they are especially meant to lead the student to consult the Etymological Dictionaries of Skeat and Kluge.

In the successive issues of the third edition of this Reader, corrections and revisions were introduced without formal notice. These changes, it was believed, did not warrant a disturbance of the practical acceptance of different issues as being the same edition. However, an indulgence in 'silent changes,' if carried too far, would needlessly occasion confusion in the use of the book in the class-room. The form in which the fourth edition is now offered to teachers and pupils will be found to be sufficiently revised to justify the specific designation, which was so nearly made appropriate by several of the revised portions of the third edition.

PREFACE.

The special feature of the present edition will be observed in the Outline of Grammar, which has been revised chiefly by changing the principal stem-terminations from the Indogermanic to the Germanic forms. The theory, represented in Professor Sievers' Grammar, that Anglo-Saxon is to be distinguished from the other Germanic languages by a peculiar retention of the Indogermanic form of stem-vowels, is set aside in conformity to the now prevailing view of scholars. This will, however, cause no difficulty in following, as before, the fuller exposition of details in Professor Sievers' Grammar (designated by S.), made available in Professor Cook's translation.

Many of the teachers who have been using this Reader have, from time to time, obligingly reported minor errors or omissions, which have all been duly considered. For this helpful kindness thankful acknowledgment is especially due Professors William H. Hulme (specifically for a collation of the manuscripts of the nineteenth selection), John S. P. Tatlock, O. F. Emerson, William Strunk, Jr., Nathaniel E. Griffin, and B. S. Monroe.

JAMES W. BRIGHT.

JOHNS HOPKINS UNIVERSITY,
March, 1917.

AN OUTLINE OF ANGLO-SAXON GRAMMAR.

INTRODUCTORY REMARKS.

1. Because of the paucity of documents in the other dialects, all introductory study of Anglo-Saxon is based on West Saxon, the language of King Alfred (871–901) and the writers who followed him until the Norman conquest. Hence the texts in this book are West Saxon and the outline of grammar gives facts only of West Saxon. Even a cursory inspection of the texts will show, however, that the usage and spelling of Alfred's time differed considerably from that of the centuries following (especially during Ælfric's time, early eleventh century and after). Hence it is necessary to distinguish between Early West-Saxon (EWS), which is analysed in the grammar, and Late West-Saxon (LWS), which is exemplified in texts xiv–xix.

The spelling of Anglo-Saxon before Alfred's reign, and to some extent after it, approached a phonetic transcription of the actual speech of the times. As most of the men who composed in the vernacular were probably accustomed to writing Latin rather than Anglo-Saxon, authors in setting down their works transcribed their pronunciations of the Anglo-Saxon words, to a considerable extent at least, with the sound values of

x *AN OUTLINE OF ANGLO-SAXON GRAMMAR.*

the Latin letters in mind, and the scribes when they copied the originals altered them to reproduce their own pronunciations in the same manner. Evidence for this conclusion is found in the divergent spellings of the various dialects and in the variant spellings, even on the same page of a West-Saxon text.[1] Because of this "phonetic" spelling, we can form a fairly exact impression of the pronunciation of Anglo-Saxon. Moreover, comparison with evidence afforded by the other Germanic dialects and that provided by Middle English and modern dialects helps to establish more precisely the sounds of the language.

Before considering the details of Anglo-Saxon pronunciation, however, it is necessary to explain some basic facts of phonetics, the science of speech-sounds. All the sounds used in speech are produced by air expelled from the lungs and later acted upon by various organs in the head and neck. From the lungs to the larynx ("Adam's Apple") the air passes without production of sound. Inside the larynx, however, are two membranes attached to its sides in such a way that they may be either stretched, so as to leave but a narrow slit between them, or relaxed, so as to leave a wide opening. In the former case, the air passing from the lungs to the mouth causes a vibration of the inner edges of the membranes, with a resulting sound commonly called "voice." In the latter case, no vibration or sound is produced. Having passed into the mouth, the air may be controlled in two ways: it may be checked

[1] In the ninth century, however, largely through Alfred's influence, the spellings of Anglo-Saxon tended to become "fixed," and after his time — even more after Ælfric's — the language had a standard spelling.

at some point and then allowed suddenly to escape (a stop, e.g., *k*) or it may encounter such a narrowing that, in forcing its way through, it produces audible friction (a continuant, e.g., *s*). Sounds so produced are called consonants. On the other hand, the air, after having produced vibration in the larynx, may encounter no such stoppage or narrowing; in such a case the air passes freely through the mouth, modified in auditory effect by the shape which the mouth takes (contrast the shape of the mouth in pronouncing the vowels in *see* and in *woe*). Sounds thus produced are called vowels. It will be observed that consonants may have voice (voiced) or not (voiceless). Indeed we have several pairs of consonant sounds which are identical except that one is voiced and the other is voiceless (*p*, *b*; *k*, *g*; *t*, *d*; *f*, *v*; *s*, *z*). On the other hand, vowels always have voice.

Aside from the broad division of stops and continuants, consonants are further classified as liquids (*l*, *r*), spirants (breathed sounds like *f* or *h*), etc. They are also characterized by the places where they are made. Thus we speak of labials (lip-consonants like *p* or *b*), dentals (teeth consonants like *d* or *t*), nasals (sounds like *m* and *n* in the production of which air passes through the nose), palatals (like *g* in *give* produced by the tongue and the hard palate) and velars (sounds produced by the tongue and the soft palate or velum, like *g* in *good*). By combining these elements we can define *m* as a voiced labial-nasal continuant, *k* as a voiceless palatal stop (in *kin*) or a voiceless velar stop (in *cool*), etc.

As we have observed, all vowels are voiced and are differentiated by the shape assumed by the mouth in

xii AN OUTLINE OF ANGLO-SAXON GRAMMAR.

pronouncing them. The mouth may be widely open as in pronouncing the a of *father*, or it may be nearly closed as in pronouncing the vowel in *see*. It may be rounded as in pronouncing the vowel in *boot*. Further, one vowel is distinguished from another by the position and tensity of the tongue. Thus in the pronunciation of *see*, the tongue is raised and tense in the front of the mouth, but in pronouncing *boot* it is raised in the back. Thus we can speak of open and closed, rounded, front and back vowels. In the following table the left side represents the front of the mouth, the right represents the back; the position at the top means a closed vowel; that at the bottom an open one. The symbols (or letters) are those used in Anglo-Saxon, and they have roughly the phonetic value of the letters in Latin.

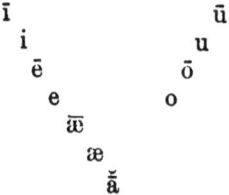

Anglo-Saxon ў̆ at first had the rounding of ŭ but the front position of ĭ; later the letter is often used to replace ĭ, an evidence that to a large extent (perhaps entirely in certain localities or among certain classes of speakers) it had lost its rounding.

A diphthong is two vowels pronounced as one syllable, e.g., the vowel sounds in *house*.

Knowledge of the elements of phonetics is of value in enabling one to understand why letters represent different sounds in different positions (see 4: (b), (c), (d), (e), (f)) and to comprehend the actual process involved

PHONOLOGY. xiii

in sound changes — e.g., the umlaut of ŭ to ў is a fronting of a back vowel, caused by a following front sound (*i* or *j*).[1]

PHONOLOGY.

ALPHABET AND PRONUNCIATION.

2. The Anglo-Saxon alphabet, as here employed, has three characters (þ, ð, æ) that are not employed in Modern English.

NOTE. — The MSS. use a special character for *w* and ʒ for *g*; 7 (= *and*) and þ̄ (= *þat*) are usual.

VOWELS AND DIPHTHONGS.

3. An approximate pronunciation of the vowels is indicated in the following table:

a   as in German *Mann*.
ā   as in English *father*.
æ   like *a* in *at, man*.
ǣ   the preceding sound lengthened.
e ⎫
ę ⎭ as in *let, men*.
ē   as in *they*.
i   as in *hit, sit, in*.
ī   as in *machine*.
o   as in German *Gott*.
ō   as in German *so*, English *boat*.
ǫ   as in *not* (Eastern U. S.).
u   as in *full, put*.
ū   as in *rule*.
y   like *ü* in German: *hübsch, Brücke*.
ȳ   as in German *grün*.

[1] *j* (pronounced like English *y*, German *j*) does not appear in Anglo-Saxon, but existed in Germanic (is found in Gothic).

xiv AN OUTLINE OF ANGLO-SAXON GRAMMAR.

ie
īe
ea
ēa
eo
ēo
io
īo
} These diphthongs (long and short) receive the stress upon the first element; the second element, being unaccented, is very much obscured in pronunciation. The sound of ea, ēa is approximately that of æ + a, ǣ + a (perhaps more nearly æ + uh); otherwise the component parts of these diphthongs are to be pronounced as indicated above.

NOTE. — The diphthongs ie, īe are peculiar to EWS, where they, however, begin to change into i, ī; in LWS the most usual representation is y, ȳ. (S. §§ 22, 31, 41, 97.)

CONSONANTS.

4. (a) The following consonants are pronounced as in Modern English: b, d, l, m, n, p, r (trilled), t, w. The pronunciation of the remaining consonants requires special attention.

(b) c has the sound of k (the symbol k occurs only exceptionally) when it precedes a back vowel (cuman), a vowel resulting from the umlaut of a back vowel (cyn) or a consonant (cwen). When it immediately precedes (cild) or follows (ic) a front vowel, it has approximately the sound of Modern English ch in choose. For instance, in the first two of the following forms c has the sound of ch; in the second two it has the sound of k: cēosan, cēas, curon, coren.

(c) f has two values. (1) In the initial and final positions, in the combinations ff, fs, ft, and in most medial positions (cf. the note below), it has the usual (voiceless) sound. (2) In the medial position between vowels and voiced consonants it has the sound of v; e.g., hlāford, ofer, sealfian, ǣfre.

PHONOLOGY. xv

Note. — In compounds like ā-fyrhtan, of-lystan, etc., f is strictly not in the medial position, and has therefore the voiceless sound.

(*d*) g has two values. (1) It almost always represents a voiced spirant, which is either velar, or palatal (like *g* in German *sagen*, or like *y* in English *you*), according to its pronunciation with velar or with palatal vowels. (2) It is pronounced like *g* in English *go* only when doubled, as in **frogga,** *frog;* and in the combination **ng**, as in English *longer*.

The combination **cg** (by origin a geminated *g*) is to be pronounced as *dg* in English *ridge*.

(*e*) h is never silent; it is pronounced (*a*) initially as in Modern English, (*b*) elsewhere as a voiceless spirant either velar (as in German *ach*) or palatal (as in German *ich*) in quality, according to the sounds with which it is combined.

(*f*) s has, in all positions, the voiceless sound, except single s between vowels, which has the voiced sound (*z*); e.g., **wesan, rīsan**, etc.

(*g*) ð and þ are used without distinction to denote the dental spirant *th*, in all positions, presumably, the voiceless spirant (as in English *thin*), except (as in the case of f) between vowels and voiced consonants where the voiced spirant (as in English *thine*) is employed; e.g., **ōðor, cweðan, weorðan**, etc.

(*h*) x = *hs*, rather than *ks*. Sc is pronounced like Modern English *sh*.

ACCENTUATION.

5. In Anglo-Saxon words are accented according to the following rules:

Rule I. — Simple words and words with formative or derivative suffixes are accented on the first syllable.

xvi AN OUTLINE OF ANGLO-SAXON GRAMMAR.

The most significant of these suffixes may receive a secondary accent.

Thus, dágas, grḗne, ḗage, ḗagena, swéotole, hélpan; swḗtèst, ðúrstìg, bódùng, léornùnga, dȳrlìng, mícelnès, wȳnsùm, glǣdlìce, bérènde, wúndrìan, wúndròde.

NOTE. — No vowels or consonants are silent; and both long and short diphthongs require the accent to be placed on the first element.

The secondary accent on suffixes is inferred from metrical usage (see the chapter on VERSIFICATION: APPENDIX II, pp. 235 ff.) and from the habits of pronunciation of modern English.

Rule II. — Compound words constitute two classes, (1) substantive compounds, and (2) verbal compounds.

A substantive compound receives the chief stress upon the first syllable of its first component (cf. Rule I); the accent of the second component is usually retained as a secondary stress.

A verbal compound is accented on the radical syllable of the verb; the prefix is therefore unaccented.

Thus, (1) substantive compounds: góld-smìð, mọ́uncỳnn, swíð-mòd (adj.), sélf-wìlles (adv.), ọ́nd-gìet, ónd-swàru, bí-gọ̀ng, bí-spèll, fór-wèard (adj.), ín-gọ̀ng, mís-dǣd, ón-gìnn, ór-èald (adj.), tṓ-wèard (adj.), ȳmbhwỳrft.

(2) Verbal compounds: ā-rísan, be-hā́tan, for-lǣ́tan, ge-bíddan, for-wéorðan, mis-fā́ran, ofer-cúman, tō-wéorpan, wið-stọ́ndan, ymb-síttan.

NOTE 1. — An important exception to *Rule II* is to be observed in the accentuation of substantive compounds with the prefixes ge-, be-, and for-; these prefixes are unaccented; e.g., ge-bód, ge-brṓðor, ge-féoht, ge-wéald; be-bód, be-gọ́ng, be-hā́t; for-gýtol (adj.), for-wýrd. That, however, these prefixes were formerly accented in substantive compounds, according to the rule, is shown by gáfol, gọ́mel, etc., in which the first element is ga-, the accented form of ge-; the accented form of be- is also left in words like bígọ̀ng, bí-spèll, bí-wìst, etc., and notice bēot < *bí-hāt,[1] by the side of the later be-hāt; and frǽ-bèorht (adj.), frǽ-mìcel, frá-coð, show a survival of the accented form of for-.

NOTE 2. — This difference in accentuation between substantive and verbal compounds (cf. English ábstract : abstráct; présent : presént;. súbject : subjéct) has (as, in part, seen above) resulted in a corresponding difference of form in certain prefixes :

ǫnd-gìet, *intelligence*	: on-gíetan, *to understand.*
ǫnd-sæ̀c, *resistance*	: on-sácan, *to resist.*
ǽf-þùnca *grudge*	: of-þýncan, *to displease.*
bi-gèng, *practice*	: be-gǫ́ngan, *to practice.*
ór-cnā̀we (adj.), *recognizable*	: ā-cnā́wan, *to know.*
ór-þònc, *device*	: ā-þę́ncan, *to devise.*
ǣð-gèng, *escape*	: oð-gǫ́ngan, *to escape.*
wíðer-sæ̀c, *hostility*	: wið-sácan, *to resist.*

PHONOLOGICAL CHANGES.

6. Anglo-Saxon is one of the group of languages obviously descended from a common ancestor, a hypothetical language called Germanic, which in turn is a member of the Indo-European family, cognate to Latin, Greek, and Sanscrit. Other members of the Germanic group are Gothic (especially important because of the early date of the writings which have been preserved), Old Norse, Old High German, Old Saxon, and Old Frisian. Detailed study shows that Anglo-Saxon belongs to a sub-group (commonly called West Germanic, which includes the three languages last named (OHG, OS, OF)), and further that it was a member of a sub-group of West Germanic (called Low German), of which Old Saxon and Old Frisian are also members.

[1] Throughout this book forms preceded by an asterisk are hypothetical reconstructions which, it is believed, once existed, but are not actually recorded.

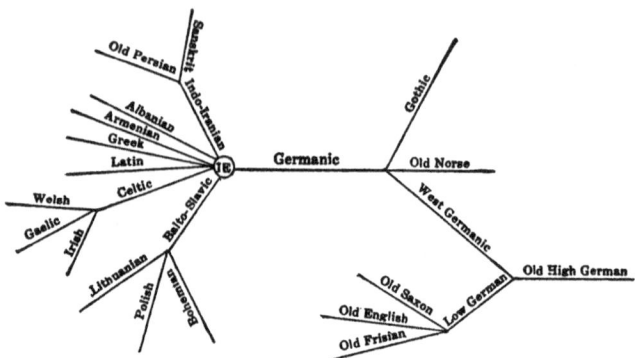

From a comparison of the words and forms of these languages, it is possible to establish the sounds and inflections that were used in Low German, in West Germanic, in Germanic, and even in Indo-European. Since change in pronunciation and forms is a constant characteristic of language, it is not surprising that West Germanic exhibits some alterations from Germanic and that Anglo-Saxon displays further changes from West Germanic. Indeed even in Germanic sound-changes occurred: thus e before n or m plus a consonant became i, and e before i or j became i.

In studying Anglo-Saxon it is necessary to observe carefully the sound-changes which occurred in it and which differentiate it from other Low German languages. In the following paragraphs the sound changes will be outlined in chronological order. The vowel changes in paragraphs 8, 9, etc. affected only vowels in accented syllables.

GEMINATION.

7. Gemination occurred in West Germanic. A single consonant (except r) when preceded by a short

vowel and followed by **j** doubled (was geminated). Later the **j** changed the quality of some of the preceding vowels, and finally it disappeared. Thus Germanic *cunja- became in West Germanic *cunnja- and finally in Anglo-Saxon cynn. Similarly *saljan became *sall-jan and finally in Anglo-Saxon sellan.

But **r** did not geminate. Hence Germanic *harja- remained unchanged in West Germanic and finally became **here** in Anglo-Saxon.

NOTE 1. — It will be noticed that geminated **f** and **g** become **bb** and **cg** respectively.

NOTE 2. — On the other hand, when the radical vowel or radical syllable is long, this formative **j**, first becoming **i** (S. §§ 45, 8), did not cause gemination of the preceding consonant.

Thus, sēc(e)an (< *sōcian), to seek; dēman (< *dōmian), to judge; sęndan (< *sǫndian), to send.

THE CHANGE OF a INTO ǫ.

8. Before a nasal consonant the vowel **a** is changed into **ǫ**. But there is no uniformity in the employment of **ǫ** for **a**. The predominant form in EWS is **ǫ**; in LWS it is **a**. (S. § 65.)

Thus, ǫnd, and; hǫnd, hand; lǫnd, land; mǫnig, manig; gǫngan, gangan; gesǫmnian, gesamnian.

NOTE. — When the preceding ǫn (< an) occurs before a voiceless spirant, **h, f, ð, s**, the nasal disappears, and, in compensation, the vowel is lengthened into **ō**. Under the same conditions, **in** and **un** become **ī** and **ū**. (S. §§ 66, 185.)

Thus, þōhte (< *þonhte), sōfte (< *sǫnfte), *softly;* tōð (< *tǫnð), *tooth;* ōðor (< *ǫnðor), *other;* gōs (< *gǫns), *goose;* sīð (Goth. sinþs), *a going;* swīð (Goth. swinþs), *strong;* mūð (Goth. munþs), *mouth*.

THE CHANGE OF a TO æ.

9. Short **a,** when not followed by a nasal, in primitive Anglo-Saxon was raised nearly, if not quite, to the position of æ. Later, according to different conditions, it appears as æ or a.

æ appears (*a*) in monosyllables except when followed by w, h, r + consonant, l + consonant, or when preceded by g, c, sc. Thus **dæg, bæc, bæd, sæd**. (*b*) in polysyllables when in prehistoric Anglo-Saxon e or i stood in the following syllable. Thus, **dæges, tōgædere, sæcce** (ds. of **sacu**), **hægel**.

a appears (*a*) when followed by w. Thus, **clawe** (gen. of **clēa**). (*b*) in polysyllables when e does not stand in the following syllable. Thus, **dagas, racu, nacod, magan, hladan, habban**. The a in past participles like **slagen** is due to the fact that earlier the ending was -an.

BREAKING.

10. (*a*) Before r + consonant, l + consonant, and h, the raised a (mentioned in **9**), e, and i are "broken" into short diphthongs, a becoming ea, and e, i, becoming eo, io. (S. §§ 77–84.)

1. Thus, a into ea: *hard > **heard**, *hard;* *half > **healf**, *half;* **wearð**, pret. sg. of **weorðan**, *to become;* **wealdan**, *to wield;* **beald**, *bold;* **feallan**, *to fall;* **heall**, *hall;* **eahta**, *eight;* **seah**, pret. sg. of **sēon**, *to see*.

2. e into eo (io) before r + consonant: **weorðan**, *to become;* **eorðe**, *earth;* **heorte**, *heart;* **weorc**, *work*.

e into eo (io) before l + consonant is restricted to l + c or h: **meolcan**, *to milk;* **seolh**, *seal*. Otherwise the e remains: **helpan**, *to help;* **swelgan**, *to swallow;* **sweltan**, *to die*.

Before h: **feohtan**, *to fight;* **teohhian**, *to arrange;* **feoh**, *cattle;* *sehan > *seohan > **sēon** (**18**).

3. i into io (eo): stem *hirdia > *hiordi > **hierde** (i-umlaut), *herdsman;* **Piht, Pioht, Peoht**, *Pict*.

PHONOLOGY. xxi

(*b*) Long vowels, especially ī, break before h:
*līht > lēoht ; *betwīh > betwēoh.

NOTE. — Breaking results from the combination of a front vowel (a, e, i) and a velar consonant (r, l, h). In passing from the pronunciation of the vowel to that of the consonant, a glide-sound is produced which is a more or less definite back vowel. One may observe this in pronouncing *well* as *wœ-al;* *there* as *thœ-ar* or *the-ur;* *fire* as *fi-ur* or *fi-or*. It is this glide-vowel that supplied the second element of these short diphthongs.

DIPHTHONGIZATION BY INITIAL PALATAL.

11. The palatals g, c, and sc, in the initial position, change a following æ into ea ; ǣ (= Germanic ē) into ēa ; and e into ie (i, y ; see 3, Note). (S. § 75.)

(*a*) Thus, æ into ea : *gæf (9) > geaf, *gave;* *gæt > geat, *got;* *cæf > ceaf, *chaff;* Lat. castra > *cæster > ceaster, *town;* *scæl > sceal, *shall;* *scæft > sceaft, *shaft;* *scær > scear, *sheared* (pret. sg.).

(*b*) ǣ into ēa : *gǣfon > gēafon, *gave* (pret. pl.); *gǣton > gēaton, *got* (pret. pl.); Lat. cāseus > *cǣsi > *cēasi > cīese (i-umlaut), *cheese;* *scǣp > scēap, *sheep;* *scǣron > scēaron, *sheared* (pret. pl.).

(*c*) e into ie (i, y): *gefan > giefan, *to give;* *getan > gietan, *to get;* *sceran > scieran, *to shear*.

NOTE 1. — Before all vowels except æ, ǣ (= Germanic ē) and e, initial g and c do not change the following vowel (S. § 76); but initial sca- and sco- frequently become scea-, sceo-; e.g., scand, sceand, scond, sceond, *shame;* pret scān, scēan, *shone;* Scottas, Sceottas, *the Scots;* scop, sceop, *poet;* scacan, sceacan, pret. scōc, scēoc, *shake;* pret. scōp, scēop, *created*.

NOTE 2. — The palatal pronunciation of medial c, cc, g, and cg, followed by a, o, or u, is often indicated by the insertion of an e (sometimes of an i). (S. § 206, 6.)

Thus, sēc(e)an (< *sōcian, S. § 45, 8 ; Goth. sōkjan), *to seek;* cwęcc(e)an (< *cwæcjan), *to quake;* męnig(e)o (< *manīgī;

xxii AN OUTLINE OF ANGLO-SAXON GRAMMAR.

Goth. **managei**), *multitude;* **bycg(e)an** (Goth. **bugjan**), *to buy;* **sęcg(e)as, sęcg(e)a, secg(i)um**, pl. of **sęcg** (stem *sægja), *man.*

NOTE 3. — The inserted letter observed in the preceding note marks with prominence the " glide " effect of palatals. This element in the pronunciation leads to further variation in the written forms. Thus, for example, for **ia** (**ja**) the graphic substitutes may be **ga, iga, igea**; for **ie** they may be **ge, ige**: **nęriau, nęrgan, nęrigan, nęrigean,** *to save;* **hęr(i)g(e)as, hęr(i)g(e)a, hęr(i)gum,** pl. of **hęre** (stem *hærja-), *army;* **wundriende, wundrigende,** *wondering;* **winig(e)a,** gen. pl. of **wine** (stem *wini-), *friend.*

Also as a graphic substitute for final **ī**, some use is made of **ig**: **bi-spell, big-spell,** *parable;* **hī, hig,** pron.; **si, sig** (Opt.), *be;* and medial **ig** is occasionally represented by **igg**: **igaŏ, iggaŏ,** *small island.* (S. § 24, Note.)

NOTE 4. — It is also to be observed that initial *jæ, *jo become **gēa, geo** (**gio**). Thus, **gēar** (< *jǣr; Goth. **jēr**), *year;* **geoc. gioc** (< *joc; Goth. **juk**), *yoke.* In like manner initial *ju becomes **geo, gio,** or is represented by **iu(io**). Thus, **geong, giong, iung**(< *jung; Goth. **juggs**), *young;* **gēo, gio, iu, io** (Goth. **ju**), *formerly.* (S. § 74.)

FINAL DOUBLE CONSONANTS.

12. Double consonants (except **cg**) at the end of a word are usually simplified. (S. § 225.)

Thus, **mǫnn, mǫn,** *man;* **męnn, męn,** *men;* **eall, eal,** *all;* **cynn, cyn,** *kin;* **będd, będ,** *bed;* **sibb, sib,** *peace.* — But, **sęcg,** *man;* **hrycg,** *ridge;* **węcg,** *wedge.*

UMLAUT (i-UMLAUT).

13. The accented vowels (radical vowels) are palatalized by an **i** or **j** of the following syllable. This species of palatalization is called **i**-umlaut, or briefly, umlaut. The **i** and **j** causing the umlaut were, for the most part, either changed into **e** or entirely lost in an early period of the language. (S. §§ 85–100.)

PHONOLOGY. xxiii

The results of umlaut may be tabulated thus:

æ (< a. 9)   becomes ę. (Sometimes æ. S.§ 89, 1, Note 1.)
ǫ (< a. 8)   becomes ę.
ā (< Germanic ai)   becomes ǣ.
ǣ (< Germanic ē)   remains ǣ.
o, ō   become e, ē.
u, ū   become y, ȳ.
ea, ēa
eo, ēo   become ie, īe; i, ī; in LWS usually y, ȳ (3, Note).
io, īo

(a) Thus, æ into ę: hęre (< stem *hærja), army; lęcgan (< *læg + jan), to lay; sęllan (< *sæl + jan), to give; męte (stem *mæti), meat.

(b) ǫ into ę: dat. sg. męn(n) (< *mǫnni), nom. (acc.) pl. męn(n) (< *mǫnniz), man; ðęnc(e)an (< *ðǫncian), to think; węndan (< *wǫndian), to turn.

(c) ā and ǣ into ǣ: dǣl (stem *dāli; Goth. dails), portion; dǣlan (< *dālian; Goth. dailjan), to share; hǣlan (< *hālian; Goth. hailjan), to heal; dǣd (stem *dǣdi; Goth. -dēds), deed; lǣce (stem *lǣcia; Goth. lēkeis), leech.

(d) o, ō into e, ē: morgen (< *morgan), but mergen (< *morgin; Goth. maurgins), morrow; dat. sg. dehter (< *dohtri), daughter; dēman (< *dōmian), to judge; fēt, tēð, gēs, dat. sg. and nom. (acc.) pl. of fōt, foot, tōð (8, Note), tooth, gōs, goose.

NOTE. — The umlaut of o (short) is restricted because o appeared in prehistoric Anglo-Saxon only rarely before i, j. Short o in I.E. became a in Germanic. Hence Germanic had no o. Later Germanic

xxiv AN OUTLINE OF ANGLO-SAXON GRAMMAR.

u when *not* followed by i, j, u, or a nasal became o. The o in forms like *morgin, *dohtri probably is due to the influence of the o in *morgan, *dohtor.

(*e*) u, ū into y, ȳ: cyning (<*cuning), *king;* cyme (stem *cumi), *a coming;* lyre (stem *luri), *loss;* gylden (<*guldin, see note under (*d*)), adj. *golden;* bycgan (Goth. bugjan), *to buy;* lȳs, mȳs, dat. sg. and nom. (acc.) pl. of mūs, *mouse*, lūs, *louse;* cȳðan (<*cūðian < *cunðian, 8, Note ; Goth. kunþjan), *to make known*.

(*f*) ea, eo, io into ie (i, y), and ēa, ēo, īo into īe (ī, ȳ): wielm, wylm (stem *wælmi>*wealmi, 10, *a*, 1), *a surging;* eald, *old*, comp. ieldra, supl. ieldesta; hierde (stem *hirdia>*heordia, 10, *a*, 3), *herdsman;* feorr, *far*, āfyrran, *to remove ;* hīeran (<*hēarian ; Goth. hausjan), *to hear;* gelīefan (<*gelēafian ; Goth. galaubjan), *to believe;* lēoht, *light*, līehtan, *to illuminate ;* frīend, fīend, dat. sg. and nom. (acc.) pl. of frīond (frēond), *friend*, fīond (fēond), *foe*.

NOTE.—In Germanic, e became i before i, j, essentially an umlaut but of far earlier date than the foregoing umlaut (cf. 6 and 87, *f*.).

u-o-a-UMLAUT.

14. In the accented syllable, and when followed by a single consonant, a may be changed into ea, and e, i into eo, io, by the influence of u, o, or a in the following syllable. This process is called u-o-a-umlaut. It is, however, not uniformly operative in the West-Saxon dialect. (S. §§ 103–109.)

Thus, **eafora**, *heir;* **heafora**, *head;* **weorold**, *world;* **heofon**, *heaven;* **metod, meotod**, *Creator;* **seofon**, *seven;* **wita, wiota**, *wise man;* **clipode, cleopode**, past of **clipian**, *to cry out* (99); **medu, medo, meodo**, *mead;* **siodu**, *custom*.

PHONOLOGY. XXV

Intervening **c** and **g** prevent the operation of this umlaut: **nacod**, adj. *naked;* **magu, mago,** *son;* **racu,** *narrative;* **sacu,** *strife;* **regol,** *rule;* **plega,** *play;* **sigor,** *victory.*

PALATAL-UMLAUT.

15. In some instances, **eo** (**io**) which resulted from the breaking of **e** before **h** (**10,** *a,* 2) becomes **ie** (**i, y**). This process presupposes the change of the velar **h**, which caused the breaking, into a palatal **h**, which then produces an effect agreeing with that of **i**-umlaut. (S. § 108.)

Thus, **reoht, rieht, riht, ryht,** *right;* **cneoht, cnieht, cniht, cnyht,** *boy;* **seox** (**x** = **hs**), **siex, six, syx,** *six.*

NOTE 1. — In LWS **ea, ēa** before **h, x, g,** and **c** are sometimes changed into **e, ē**: **sleh** (for **sleah**) imp. sg. of **slēan,** *to strike;* **seh** (for **seah**) pret. sg. of **sēon,** *to see;* **geneahhe, geneh(h)e** *enough;* **nēah, nēh,** *near;* **ðēah, ðēh,** *though;* **weaxan, wexan,** *to grow;* **bēag, bēg,** *ring;* **ēac, ēc,** *also.*

NOTE 2. — In LWS **ea, ēa** after the palatals **g, c,** and **sc** are also sometimes changed into **e, ē** (S. § 109): **gef** (for **geaf**) pret. sg. of **giefan,** *to give;* **get** (for **geat**) pret. sg. of **gietan,** *to get;* **geat, get, gate;* **gēar, gēr,** *year;* **ongēan, ongēn** *against;* **cealf, celf,** *calf;* **scēap, scēp,** *sheep.*

LOSS OF MEDIAL **g**.

16. After a front vowel, **g** (palatal) often disappears before **d** and **n**, and, in compensation, the vowel is lengthened. (S. § 214, 3.)

Thus, **bregdan, brēdan,** pret. sg. **brægd, brǣd,** *to brandish;* pret. sg. **sægde, sǣde,** pp. **gesægd, gesǣd,** of **sęcgan,** *to say;* **frignan, frīnan,** *to inquire;* **mægden, mǣden,** *maiden;* **ðegen, ðēn,** *servant;* **ðegnian, ðēnian,** *to serve;* **wægn, wǣn,** *wain.*

The occasional disappearance of **g** (velar) after a back vowel is due to the influence of palatal forms: pret. pl. **brūdon**, pp. **brōden** (for **brugdon, brogden**) follow the pattern of **bregdan, brēdan**, etc.

NOTE. — The aspirant quality of medial **g**, which underlies this process of disappearance, is further shown in the frequent change (especially in LWS) of final (and occasionally of medial) **g** into **h**. This change is most frequent after a long back vowel and after **l** and **r**, but it occurs also under other conditions. Thus, **bēag** (**bēah**), *ring;* **burg** (**burh**), *borough;* **earg** (**earh**), *cowardly;* **iergðu** (**ierhðu**), *cowardice;* **sorg** (**sorh**), *sorrow;* **flōg** (**flōh**), **lōg** (**lōh**), **slōg** (**slōh**), pret. of **flēan**, *to flay,* **lēan**, *to blame,* **slēan**, *to slay.*

LOSS OF MEDIAL h.

17. Medial **h** (not **hh**) preceded by **r** or **l** and followed by an inflectional vowel disappears, and, in compensation, the stem-vowel is lengthened. (S. § 218.)

Thus, **mearh**, gen. **mēares**, *horse;* **feorh**, gen. **fēores**, *life;* **seolh**, gen. **sēoles**, *seal.*

CONTRACTION.

18. Intervocalic **h** disappears, and the vowels thus brought together are contracted, the first vowel absorbing the second. The resulting vowels or diphthongs are long. (S. §§ 110–119, 218, 222.)

Thus, **feoh**, gen. **fēos**, *property;* **eoh**, gen. **ēos**, *horse;* **pleoh**, gen. **plēos**, *peril;* **hēah**, gen. **hēas**, and **hēan** (< *hēahan), *high.*

NOTE 1. — This disappearance of **h** also occurs sometimes before inflexional syllables beginning with **n** and **r**; before the comparative ending in **r**, and in composition: **hēah**, acc. masc. **hēane** (**hēanne**, S. § 222, Note 2), dat. fem. **hēare**, comp. **hīera** (**hierra**); **hēalic**, *high;* **plēolic**, *perilous;* **nēa-lǣcan**, *to draw near.*

NOTE 2. — Many contracted themes are due to the early loss of intervocalic **h**; for example: **slēan** (< *sleahan, 10, *a*, 1, < *slahan), *to strike*; **ðwēan** (Goth. **ðwahan**), *to wash*; **ēa** (<*aha, Goth. **ahva**, OS and OHG **aha**), *river*; **tēar** (< *tahur), *tear*; **sēon** (**sion**) (< *seohan < *sehan; Goth. **saíhvan**, OS and OHG **sehan**), *to see*; **gefēon** (< *gefehan), *to rejoice*; **twēo** (< *tweho), *doubt*; **ðēon** (< **ðīhan** (10, *b*); Goth. **þeihan** < *ðenhan), *to thrive*; **wrēon** (< *wrīhan), *to cover*; **bēot** (< *bíhāt), *boast*.

A long vowel absorbs the following vowel: **fōn** (<*fōhan < *fọnhan), *to seize*; **hōn** (< *hōhan < *họnhan), *to hang*; **tēon** (< *tēohan), *to draw*; **flēon** (< *flēohan), *to flee*.

INFLUENCE OF W.

19. The diphthongs **eo, io** produced by the breaking (**10**, *a*) or by the u-o-umlaut (**14**) of **e, i** are sometimes labialized by a preceding **w** into **u** or **o**. (S. §§ 71, 72.)

Thus, **weorðan** (**10**, *a*, 2) (<*werðan), *to become*, appears also in the form **wurðan**; **weorðian, wurðian**, *to honor*; **weorpan, wurpan**, *to throw*; **weorold** (**14**), **worold, woruld**, *world*; **sweord, swurd**, *sword*; **wita, wiota** (**14**), **weota, wuta**, *wise man*; **widuwe, wioduwe** (**14**), **wuduwe**, *widow*; **betwīh, betwēoh** (**10**, *b*), **betwuh**, with disappearance of **w, betuh**, *between*.

INFLECTION.

DECLENSION OF NOUNS.

In Indo-European, the classes of nouns differed from each other by having distinctive formative suffixes, to which were added case-endings. Thus some nouns were made of stem + o + case ending (e.g., s in the nominative, m in the accusative). Others were made by the addition of ā and case endings to the stem. A third type added i and case endings. A fourth had no vowel-suffix but added the case endings directly to the stem; a fifth used u as its suffix before the addition of the case endings. In each individual language sound-laws might change the appearance of these formative suffixes. For instance, though Greek preserves the o of the first class (e.g., logos), in Sanscrit it became a, in Latin before s and u it became u, and in Germanic it became a. Thus the -a stems of Anglo-Saxon correspond to the first declension of Latin. In the second declension Latin kept ā as ā (tabulā-), but Germanic changed it to ō. The i stems of Anglo-Saxon correspond to those third declension nouns in Latin which had -ium in the genitive plural (e.g., hostis, which is cognate to A. S. gæst). The fourth kind of nouns (consonant stems) in Latin are those nouns of the third declension which had -um in the genitive plural (e.g., rēx). The u stems of Anglo-Saxon correspond to nouns of the fourth declension in Latin. The fact that the original case endings rarely appear in Anglo-Saxon is due to the fading away of final sounds which is the result of care-

INFLECTION: DECLENSION.   xxix

less utterance, and which occurs in most languages in course of centuries; e.g., since Anglo-Saxon times final vowels in polysyllables have entirely disappeared.

THE a-DECLENSION. (S. §§ 235-250.)

20. The a-declension (which includes the stems in -ja and -wa) represents the inflection of the greater number of the masculine and the neuter nouns.

MASCULINE a-STEMS.

21. (*a*) Monosyllabic themes: **stān** (Germanic *stainas > -az; ai > ā), *stone;* **dæg,** *day;* **weal(l),** *wall;* **mearh,** *horse.*

Sing. N.A. **stān**	**dæg**	**weal(l) (12)**	**mearh**
G. **stānes**	**dæges**	**wealles (10,** *a,* **1)**	**mēares (17)**
D.I. **stāne**	**dæge**	**wealle**	**mēare**
Plur. N.A. **stānas**	**dagas (9)**	**weallas**	**mēaras**
G. **stāna**	**daga**	**wealla**	**mēara**
D.I. **stānum**	**dagum**	**weallum**	**mēarum**

NOTE. — Sing. D.I. forms without ending are found rarely, e.g., **hām, dæg.**

22. (*b*) Dissyllabic themes: **ēðel,** *property;* **engel,** *angel;* **heofon,** *heaven;* **fugol,** *bird.*

Sing. N.A. **ēðel**	**engel**	**heofon (14)**	**fugol**
G. **ēðles**	**engles**	**heofones**	**fugles**
D.I. **ēðle**	**engle**	**heofone**	**fugle**
Plur. N.A. **ēðlas**	**englas**	**heofenas**	**fuglas**
G. **ēðla**	**engla**	**heofena**	**fugla**
D.I. **ēðlum**	**englum**	**heofenum**	**fuglum**

23. (1) In the inflection of dissyllabic themes, when the radical syllable is long, the (short) middle vowel is syncopated (**ēðles, engles**); when the radical syllable is short, the middle vowel is retained (**heofones**).

(2) But certain of the themes in -el, -or, -er, -or almost regularly do not retain the middle vowel after a short radical syllable (fugles; S. § 245).

(3) A middle vowel which is long (by position) is retained: wǣfels, wǣfelses, *covering;* fǣtels, fǣtelses, *vessel;* hęngest, hęngestes, *stallion;* færeld, færeldes, *journey.*

NOTE. — There is always more or less deviation from the normal forms in the matter of the loss and the retention of the middle vowel. The middle vowel tends to assume the form e before a following a, o, u (heofones, but heofenas; S. § 129), but there is much of unregulated distribution of o and e as middle vowels.

NEUTER a-STEMS.

24. (*a*) Monosyllabic themes: gēar, *year;* word, *word;* fæt, *vessel;* lim, *limb;* feoh, *cattle.*

S. N.A. gēar (11, 4)	word	fæt	lim	feoh (fēo)
G. gēares	wordes	fætes	limes	fēos (18)
D.I. gēare	worde	fæte	lime	fēo
P. N.A. gēar	word	fatu (9)	limu, leomu (14)	
G. gēara	worda	fata	lima, leoma	
D.I. gēarum	wordum	fatum	limum, leomum	

25. The case-ending (u) of the nom. and acc. pl. disappears after a long radical syllable; after a short radical syllable it is retained: gēar, word, but fatu, limu (liomu, leomu).

NOTE. — The case-ending u of the nom. acc. pl. is often weakened to o or a. Monosyllabic themes may also have prefixes: gebed, *prayer;* gefeoht, *fight;* gewrit, *writing;* bebod, *command.*

26. (*b*) Dissyllabic themes: hēafod, *head;* nīeten (nȳten), *animal;* wǣpen, *weapon;* wæter, *water.*

INFLECTION: DECLENSION. xxxi

S. N.A. hēafod	nīeten	wǣpen	wæter
G. hēafdes	nīetenes	wǣpnes	wæteres
D.I. hēafde	nīetene	wǣpne	wætere
P. N.G. hēaf(o)du	nīetenu	wǣpnu, -en	wæter, -u
G. hēafda	nīetena	wǣpna	wætera
D.I. hēafdum	nīetenum	wǣpnum	wæterum

27. The middle vowel is generally syncopated after a long radical syllable (hēafdes, wǣpnes); it is retained after a short radical syllable (wæteres), and in some words in -en having a long radical syllable (nīetenes). The case-ending u (o, a) of the nom. acc. pl. generally remains after a long radical syllable (hēaf(o)du, nīetenu), dēoflu (-o, -a), and disappears when the radical syllable is short (wæter).

NOTE. — Usage is not uniform in the treatment of either the middle vowel or the case-ending u.

MASCULINE AND NEUTER ja-STEMS.

28. Some nouns used the suffix ja- throughout their inflection.

(a) Monosyllabic themes: Masculine, hierde, *shepherd;* here, *army;* hrycg, *ridge.* — Neuter, wīte, *punishment;* cynn, *kin.*

S. N.A. hierde (13, *f*)	here (13, *a*)	hrycg (12)	wīte	cyn(n) (12)
G. hierdes	her(i)ges (11, 3)	hrycges	wītes	cynnes
D.I. hierde	her(i)ge	hrycge	wīte	cynne
P. N.A. hierdas	her(i)g(e)as	hrycgas	wītu	cyn(n)
G. hierda	her(i)g(e)a	hrycga	wīta	cynna
D.I. hierdum	her(i)gum	hrycgum	wītum	cynnum

29. Nouns in -ja (= ia after a long radical syllable, 7, Note 2) have umlaut of the radical vowel (if it be a vowel that can be affected by umlaut), and gemination

xxxii *AN OUTLINE OF ANGLO-SAXON GRAMMAR.*

of a single consonant (except **r**) before **j** when the radical vowel is short (**7**) : stem *hrugja- > hrycg, etc.

30. (*b*) Dissyllabic themes : Masculine, **ǣfen**, *evening ;* fiscere, *fisher.* — Neuter, **wēsten**, *waste.*

S. N.A.	ǣfen	fiscere	wēsten
G.	ǣfen(n)es	fisceres	wēsten(n)es
D.I.	ǣfen(n)e	fiscere	wēsten(n)e
P. N.A.	ǣfen(n)as	fisceras	wēsten(n)u
G.	ǣfen(n)a	fiscera	wēsten(n)a
D.I.	ǣfen(n)um	fiscerum	wēsten(n)um

NOTE. — A medial geminated consonant is often simplified before an inflectional ending : **ǣfen(n)es, wēsten(n)es**, etc.

MASCULINE AND NEUTER wa-STEMS.

31. Themes: Masculine, **bearu**, *grove ;* **ðēow**, *servant.* — Neuter, **searu**, *device ;* **cnēo(w)**, *knee.*

S. N.A.	bearu, -o	ðēo(w)	searu, -o	cnēo(w)
G.	bearwes	ðēowes	searwes	cnēowes
D.I.	bearwe	ðēowe	searwe	cnēowe
P. N.A.	bearwas	ðēowas	searu, -o	cnēow(u), cnēo
G.	bearwa	ðēowa	searwa	cnēowa
D.I.	bearwum	ðēowum	searwum	cnēowum

32. (1) After a short radical syllable the **w** of the stem has become final **u** (**o**) of the theme: stem *barwa-> *baru ; gen. *barwes>bearwes (**10**, *a*, 1); the broken vowel **ea** is transferred to the theme.

(2) The **wa**-stems are relatively few in number. Some of the more common ones are : masc. **snā(w)**, *snow ;* **ðēaw**, *custom ;* — masc. and neut. **dēaw**, *dew ;* **hlāw, hlǣw**, *mound ;* **hrā(w), hrǣ(w)** *corpse ;* — neut. **bealu**, *evil ;* **mealu**, *meal ;* **hlēo(w)**, *protection ;* **trēo(w)**, *tree.*

NOTE. — A parasitic vowel, **u, o**, or **e**, is often developed before **w**: **bear(u)we, bear(o)we ; sear(u)we, sear(e)we ; beal(o)wes**, etc. (cf. **37**, Note).

INFLECTION: DECLENSION. xxxiii

THE ō-DECLENSION. (S. §§ 251-260.)

33. All nouns of the ō-declension (which includes the stems in -jō and -wō) are feminine.

ō-STEMS.

34. Themes: **giefu**, *gift*; **lār**, *lore*; **frōfor**, *consolation*; **firen**, *sin*; **costung**, *temptation*.

S. N. giefu, -o	lār	frōfor	firen	costung
G. giefe	lāre	frōfre	firene	costunga, -e
D.I. giefe	lāre	frōfre	firene	costunga, -e
A. giefe	lāre	frōfre	firene	costunga, -e
P. N.A. giefa, -e	lāra, -e	frōfra, -e	firena, -e	costunga, -e
G. giefa, -ena	lāra, -ena	frōfra	firena	costunga
D.I. giefum	lārum	frōfrum	firenum	costungum

NOTE. — Sing. D.I. forms without ending are found rarely, e.g., **strǣt**.

35. The case-ending **u** of the nom. sg. is retained only in words like **giefu** (with short radical syllable). In the gen. pl. some use is made of the case-ending **-ena**, which is taken from the n-declension (**44**). Nouns in **-ung** have commonly the case-ending **-a** in the gen. dat. acc. sg. After a long radical syllable the middle vowel is syncopated (**frōfre**); it is retained when the radical syllable is short (**firene**).

jō-STEMS.

36. Themes: **wylf**, *she-wolf*; **sib(b)**, *peace*; **byrðen**, *burden*; **hālignes**, *holiness*.

S. N. wylf	sib(b) (12)	byrðen	hālignes
G. wylfe	sibbe	byrðen(n)e	hālignesse
D.I. wylfe	sibbe	byrðen(n)e	hālignesse
A. wylfe	sibbe	byrðen(n)e	hālignesse
P. N.A. wylfa, -e	sibba, -e	byrðen(n)a, -e	hālignessa, -e
G. wylfa	sibba	byrðen(n)a	hālignessa
D.I. wylfum	sibbum	byrðen(n)um	hālignessum

xxxiv *AN OUTLINE OF ANGLO-SAXON GRAMMAR.*

Some of the more common jō-stems are: bęn(n), *wound;* blīðs, bliss, *bliss;* brycg, *bridge;* byrgen, *tomb;* cǫndel, *candle;* ęcg, *edge;* gīemen, *care;* gyden, *goddess;* hęll, *hell;* hild, *battle;* līðs, liss, *favor;* milds, milts, *mercy;* sciell, scyll, *shell;* syn(n), *sin;* wyn(n), *joy;* ȳð, *wave.*

wō-Stems.

37. Themes: stōw, *place;* beadu, *battle;* lǣs, *pasture;* mǣd, *meadow.*

S. N.	stōw	beadu	lǣs	mǣd
G.	stōwe	beadwe	lǣs(w)e	mǣd(w)e
D.I.	stōwe	beadwe	lǣs(w)e	mǣd(w)e
A.	stōwe	beadwe	lǣs(w)e	mǣd(w)e, (mǣd)
P.N.A.	stōwa, -e	beadwa, -e	lǣs(w)a, -e	mǣd(w)a, -e
G.	stōwa	beadwa	lǣs(w)a	mǣd(w)a
D.I.	stōwum	beadwum	lǣs(w)um	mǣd(w)um

Here belong also hrēow, *repentance;* trēow, *faithfulness;* nearu, *distress;* the plurals frætwa, -e, geatwa, -e, getāwa, -e, *ornaments, arms;* and ēa, *water* (<*ahu, 18, Note 2; Goth. ahwa), gen. sg. ēa (ēas, īe), dat. sg. ēa (īe, ēi), acc. sg. ēa; nom. acc. pl. ēa (ēan); dat. pl. ēaum (ēam). There is also a trace of this declension in the nom. acc. pl. clēa, clēo, dat. pl. clēam (clām), *claws.*

NOTE. — A parasitic vowel, u, o, or e, may be developed before w: bead(u)we, bead(o)we, near(o)we, geat(e)we, etc. (cf. 32, Note).

THE i-DECLENSION. (S. §§ 261-269.)

38. The i-declension includes nouns of all genders, but it has been much affected by the adoption of case-endings of the a-declension.

INFLECTION: DECLENSION.

MASCULINE AND NEUTER I-STEMS.

39. Themes : Masculine, hryre, *fall;* frēondscipe, *friendship;* pl. Dęne, *the Danes;* fęng, *grasp;* pl. Engle, *the Angles.* — Neuter, sife, *sieve.*

S. N.A.	hryre	frēondscipe	fęng	sife
G.	hryres	frēondscipes	fęnges	sifes
D.I.	hryre	frēondscipe	fęnge	sife
P. N.A.	hryras	Dęne	Ęngle	sifu
G.	hryra	Dęn(ige)a	Ęngla	sifa
D.I.	hryrum	Dęnum	Ęnglum	sifum

40. The original i of the stem has produced umlaut of the radical vowel, and survives as e in the nom. acc. sg. when the radical syllable is short: *hruri > hryre. The proper case-ending of the nom. acc. pl. masc. is e (<i), but it has been almost totally superseded by -as of the a-declension, except in proper nouns like Dęne, Ęngle, etc.

NOTE. — Traces of the original inflection of the plural are wine, *friends;* gen. pl. winigea; stęde, *places,* etc., occurring by the side of the usual forms winas, gen. winn, stędas, etc. The permanent trace of the original declension is the umlaut of the radical vowel.

FEMININE I-STEMS.

41. Themes: dǣd, *deed;* cwēn, *woman;* scyld, *guilt.*

S. N.	dǣd	cwēn	scyld
G.	dǣde	cwēne	scylde
D.I.	dǣde	cwēne	scylde
A.	dǣd (-e)	cwēn (-e)	scyld
P. N.A.	dǣde (-a)	cwēne (-a)	scylde (-a)
G.	dǣda	cwēna	scylda
D.I.	dǣdum	cwēnum	scyldum

42. The case-endings acc. sg. -e, nom. acc. pl. -a are often employed; they are adopted from the ō-declension.

xxxvi AN OUTLINE OF ANGLO-SAXON GRAMMAR.

The nouns here represented have the radical syllable long; those with a short radical syllable have conformed to the ō-declension.

THE u-DECLENSION. (S. §§ 270-275.)

43. Themes: Masculine, **sunu**, *son*. — Feminine, **hǫnd**, *hand*.

S. N.A.	sunu, -o, -a	hǫnd
G.	suna	hǫnda
D.I.	suna, -u, -o	hǫnda
P. N.A.	suna, -u, -o	hǫnda
G.	suna	hǫnda
D.I.	sunum	hǫndum

This declension has been reduced to comparatively few surviving forms, such as: masc. **wudu** (< **wiodu, 19**), gen. dat. sg. **wuda**; **sidu** (**siodu, 14**), *custom*, acc. pl. **siodo**; **medu** (**meodu, 14**), *mead*, dat. sg. **meodu, -o**; **feld**, *field*, dat. sg. **felda**; **ford**, *ford*, dat. sg. **forda**; **winter**, *winter*, dat. sg. **wintra**; **sumor**, *summer*, dat. sg. **sumera**; **weald**, dat. sg. **wealda**; — fem. **duru**, *door*, dat. sg. **duru, -a**; — neut. **fela** (**feola, 14**), *much*.

THE WEAK DECLENSION (n-DECLENSION). (S. §§ 276-278, 280.)

44. Themes: masc., **nǫma**, *name;* fem., **tunge**, *tongue;* neut., **ēage**, *eye;* masc., **gefēa**, *joy*.

S. N.	nǫma	tunge	ēage	gefēa
G.D.I.	nǫman	tungan	ēagan	gefēan
A.	nǫman	tungan	ēage	gefēan
P. N.A.	nǫman	tungan	ēagan	gefēan
G.	nǫmena	tungena	ēagena	gefēana
D.I.	nǫmum	tungum	ēagum	gefēa(u)m

45. The case-ending of the gen. pl. **-ena** (which may also occur as **-ana, -ona, -una**) is sometimes reduced to **-na**, or even to **-a** (in agreement with other declensions). **-an** often becomes **-on**.

gefēa represents a small class of stems ending in a vowel which absorbed the vowels of the case-endings. Other words of this form are: masc. **frēa**, *lord;* **lēo**, *lion,* gen. **lēon**, etc.; **twēo**, *doubt;* **ðrēa**, *threat;* — fem. **flā**, *arrow*.

ēage and **ēare**, *ear*, almost exhaust the neuter nouns of this declension.

FEMININE ABSTRACT NOUNS IN -u, -o. (S. § 279.)

46. Themes: **wlęncu**, *pride;* **stręngu** (**stręngðu, stręngð**), *strength*.

S.N.	wlęncu,-o	stręngu,-o	stręngðu,-o, stręngð
G.			
D.I.	wlęnce; -u,-o	stręnge; -u,-o	stręngðe; -u,-o
A.			
P.N.A.	wlęnc(e)a,-u,-o	stręnge,-a; -u,-o	stręngðe,-a; -u,-o
G.	wlęnc(e)a	stręnga	stręngða
D.I.	wlęncum	stręngum	stręngðum

47. These nouns represent primarily an original weak declension in **ī(n)** (e.g., **brǣdu, brǣd** = Goth. **braidei; ei = ī**); and secondarily abstracts of the ō-declension in *-iðu, (Goth. -iða): **stręngðu** < *strongiðō. The **-u** of the nom. sg. has been obtained from the ō-declension, and extended to other cases so as to produce often an uninflected singular. There is always more or less conformity to the ō-declension, especially by nouns in *-iðu. (S. § 255, 3.)

MINOR DECLENSIONS.

THE r-DECLENSION. (S. § 285.)

48. Themes (nouns of relationship): **fæder**, *father;* **mōdor**, *mother;* **brōðor**, *brother;* **sweostor**, *sister;* **dohtor**, *daughter*.

S. N.A. fæder	mōdor, -ur, -er	brōðor, -ur, -er
G. fæder, -(e)res	mōdor (mēder)	brōðor
D.I. fæder	mēder (13, *d*)	brēðer (13, *d*)
P. N.A. fæd(e)ras	mōdru, -a	brōðor, -ðru
G. fæd(e)ra	mōdra	brōðra
D.I. fæd(e)rum	mōdrum	brōðrum

S. N.A. sweostor, -ur, -er	dohtor, -ur, -er
G. sweostor	dohtor (dehter)
D.I. sweostor	dohtor, dehter (13, *d*)
P. N.A. sweostor, -tru, -tra	dohtor, -tru, -tra
G. sweostra	dohtra
D.I. sweostrum	dohtrum

The datives **mēder, dehter** (which are sometimes transferred into the genitive) exhibit umlaut of the radical vowel (**mēder** < *mōdri; **dehter** < *dohtri (**13**, note)). **sweostor** also becomes **swoster, swuster** (**19**), **swyster**.

Here belong also the collective plurals **gebrōðor**, *brethren*, **gesweostor**, *sisters*.

THE nd-DECLENSION. (S. § 286.)

49. Themes: **frēond**, *friend;* **hęttend**, *enemy*.

S. N.A. frēond	hęttend
G. frēondes	hęttendes
D.I. friend (13, *f*), frēonde	hęttende
P. N.A. friend, frēond, frēondas	hęttend, das, -de
G. frēonda	hęttendra
D.I. frēondum	hęttendum

INFLECTION: DECLENSION. xxxix

50. This declension comprises masculine nouns of agency derived from present participles. Like **frēond** are declined **fēond,** *foe;* the collective plurals **gefrīend,** *friends;* **gefīend,** *foes.* Like **hęttend** are declined **āgend,** *owner;* **dēmend,** *judge;* **ēhtend,** *persecutor;* **fultum(i)end,** *helper;* **gōddōnd** (pl. **gōddēnd**), *bene⋅factor;* **healdend,** *keeper;* **hǣlend, nęrgend,** *saviour;* **wealdend,** *ruler;* **wīgend,** *warrior;* etc. The case-endings gen. sg. -es, dat. sg. -e, nom. pl. -as show conformity to the a-declension, and nom. pl. -e, gen. pl. -ra are analogical forms derived from the regular strong adjective inflection of present participles (**62**).

THE **er**-DECLENSION (Goth. **is**-, Indogerm. **os**-**es**- declension). (S. §§ 280-299.)

51. Themes: Neuter, **lǫmb,** *lamb;* **cealf,** *calf;* **ǣg,** *egg.*

S. N.A.	lǫmb	cealf	ǣg
G.	lǫmbes	cealfes	ǣges
D.I.	lǫmbe	cealfe	ǣge
P. N.A.	lǫmbru, lǫmber, lǫmb	cealfru	ǣgru
G.	lǫmbra lǫmba	cealfra	ǣgra
D.I.	lǫmbrum lǫmbum	cealfrum	ǣgrum

The plurals in **r**, given in the paradigms, to which may be added the occasional pl. **cildru,** *children,* conserve notable traces of the primitive stem-formation.

52. The original stem-endings are also to be recognized in themes like **dōgor,** *day;* **sigor,** *victory;* **hrȳðer,** *cattle;* but these have adopted the a-declension, and often a change of gender. Sometimes **-er** is reduced to **-e,** as in **sige** (< *****siger**; Goth. **sigis**), *victory;* **ęge**

AN OUTLINE OF ANGLO-SAXON GRAMMAR.

(Goth. **agis**), *fear*, and such words have generally become masculine and follow the i-declension. Otherwise the total loss of the stem-ending (as in the sing. of the paradigms) has resulted in a theme like **sæl**, *hall* (by the side of **salor**).

THE RADICAL CONSONANT DECLENSION. (S. §§ 281-284.)

53. Themes: Masculine, **mǫnn**, *man;* **fōt**, *foot;* **tōð**, *tooth.* — Feminine, **bōc**, *book;* **burg**, *borough.*

S. N.A.	mǫn(n)	fōt	tōð	bōc	burg
G.	mǫnnes	fōtes	tōðes	bēc, bōce	byr(i)g (13, *e*)
D.I.	męn(n)(13, *b*)	fēt (13, *d*)	tēð	bēc	byr(i)g
P. N.A.	męn(n)	fēt	tēð	bēc	byr(i)g
G.	mǫnna	fōta	tōða	bōca	burga
D.I.	mǫnnum	fōtum	tōðum	bōcum	burgum

54. (1) A weak acc. sg. **mǫnnan**, and the pl. **fōtas**, **tōðas** sometimes occur. Other masculine forms of this declension survive in **hæle** (**hæleð**), *hero*, pl. **hæle**, **hæleð** (by the side of **hæleðas**); **mōnað**, *month*, pl. **mōnað** (by the side of **mōn(e)ðas**). There are also the neuter forms: **scrūd**, *garment*, dat. sg. **scrȳd**; **ealu**, *ale*, gen. dat. sg. **ealoð**, **-að**.

(2) Like **bōc** are also declined the feminines **brōc**, *breeches*, pl. **brēc**; **gāt**, *goat*, pl. **gēt**; **gōs**, *goose*, pl. **gēs**; **lūs**, *louse*, pl. **lȳs**; **mūs**, *mouse*, pl. **mȳs**; **cū**, *cow* (gen. **cū(e)**, **cȳ**, **cūs**; dat. **cȳ**; pl. nom. acc. **cȳ(e)**, gen. **cū(n)a**, **cȳna**; dat. **cūum**, **cūm**). — **niht**, *night*, preserves a trace of this declension in dat. sg., nom. acc. pl. **niht** (the adverbial gen. **nihtes** (**70**) is due to association with **dæges**); and **mægeð**, **mægð**, *maid*, in

INFLECTION: DECLENSION. xli

undergoing no change in the sing. and the nom. acc. pl. — **burg** sometimes shows departure from this declension by the gen. dat. sg. **burge**, nom. acc. pl. **burge, -a**.

ADJECTIVES.

DECLENSION OF ADJECTIVES. (S. §§ 291–304.)

55. Adjectives have a double inflection: (1) the Strong (or Indefinite), and (2) the Weak (or Definite) declension.

(1) The Strong declension is used whenever none of the conditions for the use of the Weak declension is present. It has some special case-endings, which are of pronominal origin: masc. neut. dat. sg. **-um**: masc. acc. sg. **-ne**; fem. gen. dat. sg. **-re**; masc. nom. acc. pl. **-e**; gen. pl. **-ra**; with these exceptions this declension agrees with that of **a-** (**ja-, wa-**) stems for the masc. and neut., and with that of **ō-** (**jō-, wō-**) stems for the fem. forms. A few traces are all that is left to represent the declension of **i-** and **u-**stems (**59, 2, 3**).

(2) The Weak declension is used when the adjective is preceded by a demonstrative (sometimes a possessive) pronoun; in direct address (vocative); and in poetry sometimes in place of the Strong declension. Moreover, the comparatives always follow this declension, and usually the superlatives; and all the ordinals (except **ǣrest, fyrmest, fyrest, fyrst,** *first,* which are declined both strong and weak; and **ōðor,** *second,* which is declined strong only. **74, 7**).

This declension agrees throughout with the **n**-declension of nouns (**44**), except that the gen. pl. often ends in **-ra**.

STRONG DECLENSION OF ADJECTIVES.

(a) a- (ō-) STEMS.

56. Themes: **hræd**, *rapid;* **gōd**, *good.*

	MASCULINE.	NEUTER.	FEMININE.
S. N.	hræd	hræd	hradu, -o
G.	hrædes	hrædes	*hrædre* (9)
D.	*hradum* (9)	*hradum*	*hrædre*
A.	*hrædne*	hræd	hræde
I.	hræde	hræde	
P. N.A.	*hræde*	hradu, -o; -e	hrada, -e
G.	*hrædra*	*hrædra*	*hrædra*
D.I.	**hradum**	hradum	hradum

	MASCULINE.	NEUTER.	FEMININE.
S. N.	gōd	gōd	gōd
G.	gōdes	gōdes	gōdre
D.	gōdum	gōdum	gōdre
A.	gōdne	gōd	gōde
I.	gōde	gōde	
P. N.A.	gōde	gōd; -e	gōda, -e
G.	gōdra	gōdra	gōdra
D.I.	gōdum	gōdum	gōdum

NOTE.—The special case-endings, of pronominal origin (55,1), are marked by difference of type in the paradigm of **hræd**.

57. (1) In LWS the nom. acc. pl. neut. generally ends in -e (in conformity to the masc.); the cases in -um sometimes appear in -on, -an; and -re, -ra may become -ere, -era.

NOTE.—The nom. acc. pl. masc. **fēawe**, *few*, and **manege**, *many*, because of association with the noun **fela**, *much* (which is also used as an adjective), frequently become **fēawa** and **manega**; so too may occur fem. **maniga**; **ealla** for **ealle**, *all;* and **āna** for **āne**, *alone.*

(2) Adjectives in ·h: **hēah**, *high*, fem. **hēah**, **hēa**; gen. **hēas** (**18**), LWS also **hēages**; fem. gen. dat.

INFLECTION: DECLENSION. xliii

hēare, hēahre, hēarre; dat. hēaum, hēam, hēagum; acc. masc. hēanne, hēane, hēahne, etc. — hrēoh, *rough;* dat. hrēoum; acc. masc. hrēone; gen. pl. hrēora; etc. — rūh, *rough*, gen. rūwes, rūges; acc. masc. rūhne: etc. — ðwēorh, *transverse*, gen. ðwēores; etc. — wōh, *wrong*, gen. wōs, wōges; etc.

(3) In the declension of dissyllabic themes the same principles generally prevail in the retention and the loss of the middle vowels which have been observed in the corresponding declensions of nouns.

(b) ja- (jō-) AND wa- (wō-) STEMS.

58. Themes: ja- (jō-) theme, **grēne**, *green;* wo- (wō-) theme, **gearu**, *ready*.

	MASCULINE.	NEUTER.	FEMININE.
S. N.	grēne	grēne	grēnu, -o
G.	grēnes	grēnes	grēnre
D.	grēnum	grēnum	grēnre
A.	grēnne	grēne	grēne
I.	grēne	grēne	
P. N. A.	grēne	grēnu, -o; -e	grēna, -e
G.	grēnra	grēnra	grēnra
D. I.	grēnum	grēnum	grēnum

	MASCULINE.	NEUTER.	FEMININE.
S. N.	gearu, -o	gearu, -o	gearu, -o
G.	gearwes		gear(o)re
D.	gearwum		gear(o)re
A.	gearone	gearu, -o	gearwe
I.	gearwe		
P. N. A.	gearwe	gearu; -we	gearwa, -e
G.		gear(o)ra	
D. I.		gearwum	

59. (1) frīo (frēo, frīoh, frēoh), *free* (stem *frija-), gen. **friges**; dat. **frigum**; pl. **frige**, etc., has also contracted forms: dat. **frīoum**; gen. dat. fem. **frīore**; acc. masc. **frīone**; pl. **frīo**; gen. **frīora**, etc.

NOTE. — The **wa**-stems often exhibit a parasitic vowel before **w**: **gear(o)wes, gear(e)wes, gear(u)we**, etc. (cf. 32, Note).

(2) Adjective **i**-stems follow the declension of **grēne** (**ja**-stem). Thus, **bryce** (stem **bruci*; 13, *e*), *fragile*; **gemyne**, *mindful;* **swice**, *deceitful.* — With long radical syllable: **brȳce**, *useful;* **blīðe**, *blithe;* **swēte**, *sweet.*

(3) Adjective **u**-stems have adopted either the **a**- or the **ja**-declension. **c(w)icu, c(w)ucu** (< **cwiocu** : 19), *alive*, and **wlacu**, *tepid*, have the appearance of relics of the **u**-declension, but strictly belong to the **wa**-stems.

WEAK DECLENSION OF ADJECTIVES.

60. Theme: **gōd**, *good*.

	MASCULINE.	NEUTER.	FEMININE.
S. N.V.	gōda	gōde	gōde
G.	gōdan	gōdan	gōdan
D.I.	gōdan	gōdan	gōdan
A.	gōdan	gōde	gōdan

	ALL GENDERS.
P. N.V.A.	gōdan
G.	gōdena, -ra (55, 2)
D.I.	gōdum

NOTE 1. — The gen. pl. sometimes occurs in **-ana, -an** (conforming to the other cases); or in **-na**, and **-a** (conforming to nouns). The case-ending **-an** sometimes appears as **-on**; and **-um** may become **-an, -on**.

NOTE 2. — Adjectives in **h** are contracted: **hēah**, *high;* **hēa, hēan** (18), etc. — **ðwēorh**, *transverse:* **ðwēora, -e**, etc.; **wōh**, *wrong:* gen. pl. **wōna**, etc.

INFLECTION: DECLENSION. xlv

DECLENSION OF PARTICIPLES. (S. §§ 305, 306.)

61. Participles admit of the double inflection of adjectives. When the strong inflection is employed, the present participle is declined like a **ja-** (**jō**) stem (**58, grēne**); the past participles (of both Strong and Weak verbs) are declined like **a-** (**ō-**) stems (**56**).

STRONG DECLENSION OF THE PRESENT PARTICIPLE.

62. Theme: Present Participle, **singende**, *singing*.

	MASCULINE.	NEUTER.	FEMININE.
S. N.	singende	singende	singendu, -o
G.	singendes	singendes	singendre
D.	singendum	singendum	singendre
A.	singendne	singende	singende
I.	singende	singende	
P. N.A.	singende	singendu, -o ; -e	singenda, -e
G.	singendra	singendra	singendra
D.I.	singendum	singendum	singendum

NOTE. — The acc. sg. masc. is often uninflected (having the ending -e, instead of -ne).

COMPARISON OF ADJECTIVES. (S. §§ 307–314.)

63. (1) An adjective forms its Comparative in the ending **-ra** (< *-**ira** and *-**ora** = Goth. -**iza** and -**oza**); its Superlative in **-est**, or **-ost** (= Goth. -**ist**, -**ost**). There may be umlaut of the radical vowel, but in most instances umlaut does not occur.

Thus, (*a*) with umlaut:

| eald, *old* | ieldra | ieldest |
| ēaðe, *easy* | ieðra | ieðest |

geong, *young*	giengra	giengest
grēat, *great*	grīetra	grīetest
hēah, *high*	hīehra (hierra)	hīeh(e)st
lǫng, *long*	lęngra	lęngest
sceort, *short*	sciertra	sciertest

(b) Without umlaut:

ceald, *cold*	cealdra	cealdost
earm, *poor*	earmra	earmost
heard, *hard*	heardra	heardost
hlūd, *loud*	hlūdra	hlūdost
lēof, *dear*	lēofra	lēofost
rīce, *powerful*	rīcra	rīcost
swīð, *strong*	swīðra	swīðost
swift, *swift*	swiftra	swiftost

(2) In the limited class of umlauted forms the original endings were -ira, -ist; while the more common absence of umlaut proves the preference for -ora, -ost.

NOTE 1. — It is because comparatives follow the weak declension (55, 2) that the masculine theme (in -a) is adopted as the theme of the comparative; superlatives admit of double inflection, therefore the strong theme is here employed (in -ist, -ost, not -ista, -osta).

NOTE 2. — The ending -ost (which is often represented by -ust, -ast) is occasionally transferred to umlauted forms; and -est is often found with the unumlauted forms, particularly when these are inflected: heardesta, rīcestan, etc.

64. Some few comparatives and superlatives have no positive, but are based on corresponding adverbs or prepositions:

(nēah, *near*)	nēarra	nīehst
(ǣr, *earlier*)	ǣrra	ǣrest
(fore, *before*)	furðra	fyr(e)st

INFLECTION: DECLENSION. xlvii

65. A trace of superlatives in -m survives in **forma,** *the first,* and **hindema,** *the hindmost.* But to this -m the regular ending -est has been joined; the result is a (double) superlative ending -mest (-mæst; = Goth. -m-ist-), which appears in the following list. These adjectives are, in the greater number of instances, also based upon adverbs or prepositions, and usually have the comparative in -erra.

(sīð, *late*)	sīðra	sīðemest, sīðest
læt, *late*	lætra	lætemest, lætest
(inne, *within*)	inn(er)ra	innemest
(ūte, *without*)	ūt(er)ra, ȳtrra	ȳtemest, ūtemest
(ufan, *above*)	uferra, yfer(r)a	yf(e)mest, ufemest
(niðan, *below*)	niðerra	niðemest
(fore, *before*)	furðra	fyrmest, forma
(æfter, *after*)	æfterra	æftemest
mid(d), *mid*		mid(e)mest
(norð, *northward*)	norð(er)ra, nyrðra	norðmest
(sūð, *southward*)	sūð(er)ra, sȳðerra	sūðmest
(ēast, *eastward*)	ēast(er)ra	ēastmest
(west, *westward*)	(west(er)ra)	westmest

66. In the following list the root of the comparative and superlative differs from that of the positive.

gōd, *good*	bet(e)ra, bettra	bet(e)st
yfel, *evil*	wiersa	wierrest, wierst
micel, *great*	māra, mǣrra	mǣst
lȳtel (lȳt), *little*	lǣssa	lǣs(e)st, lǣrest

NOTE.—With **gōd** is to be associated (in meaning) the adv. **sēl,** *better,* comp. adj. **sēlla, sēlra,** superl. adj. **sēlost, sēlest;** and the adv. and subst. **mā (mǣ),** *more,* belongs to **māra.**

AN OUTLINE OF ANGLO-SAXON GRAMMAR.

ADVERBS.

CLASSIFICATION AND FORMATION OF ADVERBS.
(S. §§ 315-321.)

67. Some of the more important adverbs of place are the following: —

hwǽr (LWS hwār), *where*	hwider, *whither*	hwǫnan, *whence*
ðǽr (LWS ðār), *there*	ðider, ðidres, *thither*	ðǫnan, *thence*
hēr, *here*	hider, hidres, *hither*	heonan, *hence*
inne, innan, *within*	in(n)	innan
ūte, ūtan, *without*	ūt	ūtan
uppe, uppan, *up, above*	up(p)	uppan
ufan, *above*		ufan
neoðan, *below, beneath*	niðor	neoðan
foran, *before*	forð	foran
hindan, *behind*	hinder	hindan
	ēast, *east*	ēastan
	west, *west*	westan
	norð, *north*	norðan
	sūð, *south*	sūðan
feorran, *far*	feor(r)	feorran
nēah (nēh), *near*	nēar	nēan

ADVERBS FORMED FROM ADJECTIVES AND NOUNS.

68. (1) Many adverbs in their formation have a definite relation either to adjectives or to nouns. The largest class is derived from adjectives by the addition of the abverbial ending -e, which originally was the case-ending of the instrumental locative singular of nouns. Adjectives in -e remain unchanged.

Thus, adj. **georn**, *eager*, — adv. **georne**; **hlūd**, *loud*, — **hlūde**; **hlūtor**, *clear*, — **hlūtre**; **lǫng**, *long*, — **lǫnge**; **dēop**, **dēoplīc**, *deep*, — **dēope**, **dēoplīce**; **glæd**, **glædlīc**, *glad*, etc. — **glædlīce**. — From adjectives in -e : adj. **blīðe**, *joyful*, — adv. **blīðe**; **clǽne**, *clean*, — **clǽne**.

INFLECTION: DECLENSION.

NOTE 1. — In consequence of a marked preference for the termination -līce, these adverbs come to exceed in number adjectives in -līc.

NOTE 2. — The adverbs sōfte, swōte are without the umlaut of the corresponding adjectives sēfte, *soft*, swēte, *sweet*.

69. Other adverbial endings are -a and -unga (-enga, -inga).

Thus: gēara, *of yore* (= gen. pl. of gēar, *year*); sōna, *soon;* tela (teola, teala, tala), *properly;* tūwa (twūwa, twīwa), *twice;* ðrīwa, *thrice.* — æninga (āninga, ānunga), *entirely;* eallunga (eallinga), *altogether;* grundlunga (grundlinga), *completely;* sęmnunga (sęmninga), *suddenly;* wēninga, *perhaps.*

70. Oblique cases of nouns and adjectives are used adverbially, and from these, as well as from prepositional phrases, have sprung more or less permanent adverbial forms:

Thus (*a*) genitive adverbs: dæges, *by day;* nihtes, *by night;* ealles, *altogether;* nealles (= nā + ealles; nālles, nālas, nālæs, nāls), *not at all;* ęlles, *otherwise;* micles, *very;* nēades, *needs;* simbles, singales, *always;* willes, gewealdes, *willingly;* self-willes, *voluntarily;* up-weardes, *upwards;* tōgegnes, *against;* ungewisses, *unconsciously;* hū gēares, *at what time of year;* nēde (fem.), *necessarily.*

(*b*) Accusative adverbs: fyrn, gefyrn, *formerly;* full, *fully;* genōg, *enough;* hwōn, *somewhat;* lȳtel, lȳt, *little;* ungemęt, *immoderately;* upweard, *upward.*

(*c*) Dative (Instr.) adverbs: hwēne (instr.), *somewhat;* hām (hāme), *home;* sāre, *sorely;* hwīlum, *sometimes;* stundmǣlum, *time after time;* lȳtlum, *little;* miclum, *very.*

AN OUTLINE OF ANGLO-SAXON GRAMMAR.

COMPARISON OF ADVERBS. (S. §§ 322, 323.)

71. Adverbs (chiefly those which are derived from adjectives) adopt the comparative and superlative endings -or, -ost (-ust, -ast): geórne, *eagerly;* geornor, geornost.

72. Certain monosyllabic comparatives are without the comparative ending; these were originally in -iz (= Goth. -is), and have therefore umlaut: ǣr, *earlier* (< *āriz < *airiz, Goth. airis); bęt, *better* (< *batiz, Goth. batis); ęnd, *formerly;* fierr, *farther;* īeð (ēað), *easier;* lǣs, *less;* lęng, *longer;* mǣ (mā), *more;* nȳr (nēar), *nearer;* sēft, *softer;* sēl, *better;* sīð, *later;* tylg, *more willingly*.

NUMERALS.

CARDINAL AND ORDINAL NUMERALS. (S. §§ 324–331.)

73. The cardinal and the ordinal numerals are as follows: —

	CARDINAL.	ORDINAL.
1	ān	forma, formesta, fyrmest / fyrest, fyrst; ǣrest
2	twēgen, tū, twā	ōðer, æfterra
3	ðrie, ðrīo (ðrēo)	ðridda
4	fīower (fēower)	fēowerða, fēorða
5	fīf	fīfta
6	siex, six	siexta
7	siofon (seofon)	seofoða, -eða
8	eahta	eahtoða, -eða, -eoða
9	nigon	nigoða, -eða, -eoða
10	tīen, tȳn	tēoða
11	ęndlefan, -leofan, -lufan, etc.	ęndlefta, ęllefta, etc.
12	twęlf	twęlfta

INFLECTION: DECLENSION. li

	CARDINAL.	ORDINAL.
13	ðrēotīene, -tēne, -tȳne	ðrēotēoða
14	fēowertīene	fēowertēoða
15	fīftīene	fīftēoða
16	siextīene	siextēoða
17	seofontīene	seofontēoða
18	eahtatīene	eahtatēoða
19	nigontīene	nigontēoða
20	twēntig	twēntigoða, -tigða, -tiga, etc.
21	ān ǫnd twēntig	ān ǫnd twēntigoða
30	ðritig	ðrītigoða
40	fēowertig	fēowertigoða
50	fīftig	fīftigoða
60	siextig	siextigoða
70	(hund)seofontig	(hund)seofontigoða
80	(hund)eahtatig	(hund)eahtigoða
90	(hund)nigontig	(hund)nigontigoða
100	hundtēontig, hund, hundred	(hundtēontigoða)
110	hundęndlefantig hundǣlleftig, etc.	(hund)ęndleftigoða
120	hundtwęlftig	(hund)twęlftigoða
200	twā (tū) hund	
1000	ðūsend	

DECLENSION OF NUMERALS.

74. (1) The cardinal **ān**, *one*, is generally declined like a strong adjective, with the acc. sg. masc. **ǣnne, ānne**, and the instr. sg. **ǣne, āne**. When it signifies *alone*, it is often declined weak. (See also the Indefinite Pronouns.)

(2) Themes: **twēgen**, *twain, two;* **ðrīe**, *three*.

	MASCULINE.	NEUTER.	FEMININE.
N. A.	twēgen	tū, twā	twā
G.		twēg(e)a, twēgra	
D.		twǣm, twām	

AN OUTLINE OF ANGLO-SAXON GRAMMAR.

	MASCULINE.	NEUTER.	FEMININE.
N. A.	ðrie, ðrī (ðrȳ)	ðrio, ðrēo	ðrio, ðrēo
G.		ðriora, ðrēora	
D.		ðrim	

(3) Like **twēgen** is declined **bēgen** (**beggen**), *both;* neut. **bū**; fem. **bā**; gen. **bēg(r)a**; dat. **bǣm, bām**.

Note.—There is more or less disregard of gender in the use of the above forms. The fem. **twā**, which has been extended to the neut., is sometimes used for **twēgen**; and **bā** and **bū** for **bēgen**, and **ðrēo** for **ðrīe**, occur. When nouns of different gender are referred to, the neut. form of the numeral is generally employed. There is a tendency to use conjointly the monosyllabic forms of **twēgen** and **bēgen**, with some freedom as to gender: masc. fem. **bā twā**; neut. (also masc. fem.) **būtū, būtā**, *both.*

(4) The cardinals from 4 to 19 are, as a rule, not inflected, except when they are used absolutely (i.e. without a noun); they then take the case-endings nom. acc. -e, gen. -a, dat. -um.

(5) The cardinals in -tig are often not inflected; when inflected, the case-endings are gen. -a, -ra, dat. -um, and sometimes gen. sg. -es.

(6) **hund**, usually uninflected, has the dat. sg. **hunde**, and the nom. acc. pl. **hunde**, dat. pl. **hundum**. When inflected, **hundred** has the following case-endings: gen. sg. -es, dat. sg. -e; nom. acc. pl. -u, -o; gen. pl. -a, dat. pl. -um. The same case-endings with the addition of gen. pl. -ra occur with **ðūsend**.

(7) The ordinals are all declined like weak adjectives, except **ǣrest, fyrmest, fyrest, fyrst**, which conform to both the strong and the weak declension, and **ōðer** which conforms to the strong declension only.

INFLECTION: DECLENSION.   liii

PRONOUNS.

PERSONAL PRONOUNS. (S. §§ 332-334.)

75. Themes: First Person, ic, *I;* Second Person, ðū, *thou;* Third Person, hē, *he,* hit, *it,* hēo, *she.*

	Sing. N.	ic	ðū
	G.	mīn	ðīn
	D.	mē	ðē
	A.	mec, mē	ðec, ðē
	Dual N.	wit	git
	G.	uncer	incer
	D.	unc	inc
	A.	uncit, unc	incit, inc
	Plur. N.	wē	gē
	G.	ūser, ūre	ēower (īower)
	D.	ūs	ēow (īow)
	A.	ūsic, ūs	ēowic, ēow (iow)

S. N.	hē	hit	hēo (hio), hie, hī
G.	his	his	hiere, hire, hyre
D.	him	him	hiere, hire, hyre
A.	hiene, hine	hit	hie, hī (hig), hēo
P. N.A.		hie, hī (hig), hȳ, hēo (hio)	
G.		hiera, hira, hyra, heora (hiora)	
D.		him, heom	

NOTE. — The Personal Pronouns are also used as Reflexives.

POSSESSIVE PRONOUNS. (S. §§ 335, 336.)

76. The Possessive Pronouns mīn, *mine;* ðīn, *thine;* ūre, *our;* ēower, *your;* sīn, *his, her, its;* uncer, *of us two;* incer, *of you two,* are declined like adjectives (strong declension).

NOTE. — The genitives of the Third Personal Pronouns are often used as Possessives.

DEMONSTRATIVE PRONOUNS. (S. §§ 337–339.)

77. Themes: masc., sē, neut., ðæt, fem., sēo, *the, that;* — masc., ðēs, neut., ðis, fem., ðēos, *this.*

S. N.	sē	ðæt	sēo (sīo)
G.	ðæs	ðæs	ðǣre
D.	ðǣm, ðām	ðǣm, ðām	ðǣre
A.	ðone (ðane, ðæne)	ðæt	ðā
I.	ðȳ, ðē, ðon	ðȳ, ðē, ðon	
P. N.A.		ðā	
G.		ðāra, ðǣra	
D.I.		ðǣm, ðām	

S. N.	ðēs	ðis	ðēos (ðīos)
G.	ðis(s)es, ðys(s)es		ðisse, ðeosse (ðisre)
D.	ðis(s)um, ðys(s)um, ðeosum		ðisse, ðeosse (ðisre)
A.	ðisne, ðysne	ðis	ðās
I.	ðȳs, ðis		
P. N.A.		ðās	
G.		ðissa, ðeossa (ðissera)	
D.I.		ðis(s)um, ðys(s)um, ðeos(s)um	

The Demonstrative **ilca**, *the same*, is generally declined like a weak adjective; **self (seolf, silf, sylf)**, *self*, conforms to both declensions of the adjective.

RELATIVE PRONOUNS. (S. § 340.)

78. There is no inflected Relative Pronoun. This want is supplied by the use of the Relative Particle ðe, used either alone or in combination with the weaker demonstrative sē, ðæt, sēo (and sometimes in combination with a Personal Pronoun), and by the relative use of this demonstrative.

INFLECTION: DECLENSION. lv

INTERROGATIVE PRONOUNS. (S. §§ 341, 342.)

79. Theme: masc., **hwā**, *who?* neut., **hwæt**, *what?*

S. N.	hwā	hwæt
G.	hwæs	hwæs
D.	hwǣm, hwām	hwǣm, hwām
A.	hwone (hwane, hwæne)	hwæt
I.	hwī, hwȳ, hwon (hwan)	hwī, hwȳ, hwon (hwan)

NOTE. — There are no special feminine forms. The instrumental case has also yielded the adverb **hū**, *how?*

hwæðer, *which of two?* **hwilc** (**hwylc, hwelc**), *which?* **hūlic**, *what sort?* are declined like strong adjectives.

INDEFINITE PRONOUNS. (S. §§ 343-349.)

80. (1) The Indefinites **ǣlc**, *each;* **ān**, *a, an;* **ǣnig**, *any;* **nǣnig** (< **ne + ǣnig**), *none;* **ōðer**, *other;* **sum**, *certain;* **swilc**, *such*, are declined like strong adjectives. The nom. sg. **mǫn** (*man*) is used as an indefinite, *one*.

(2) The Interrogatives **hwā, hwæðer** and **hwilc** are often used as Indefinites. They are also made indefinite by the use of **swā**, *so:* **swā hwā swā**, *who(so)ever;* **swā hwæðer swā**, *which(so)ever of two*, etc. Moreover, the Interrogatives in composition yield many Indefinites: **āhwā**, *any one;* **āhwæt**, *anything;* **ǣghwā, æthwā, gehwā**, *each, every;* **āhwæðer** (**ōhwæðer, āwðer, ōwðer, āðer, ōðer**); **ǣghwæðer** (**ǣgðer, āðer**), *either, each.* **nāhwæðer**, *neither;* **ǣghwilc, gehwilc**, *each;* **sǫmhwylc**, *some one;* with the indeclinable **-hwega** (**-hwegu, -hwuga, -u**, etc.): **hwæthwega**, *something;* **hwilchwega**, *any one;* and **æthwega**, *somewhat*.

(3) Other substantival indefinites are: **āwiht** (**āwuht, āuht, āht; ōwiht, ōwuht, ōht**), *anything;* **nāwiht** (**nāuht, nāht, nōht**, etc.) and **nānwuht**, *nothing*.

CONJUGATION.

GENERAL CLASSIFICATION OF VERBS.

81. (1) The two comprehensive classes of verbs are: (1) Strong Verbs, those which form the Principal Parts with a variation of the radical vowel (*Ablaut*); and (2) Weak Verbs, those which (without ablaut) form the Preterit and Past Participle in **d (t)**.

(2) The Principal Parts of a verb are the Infinitive (which contains that form of the radical vowel which is employed in the entire system of the present tense), the Preterit Singular (and, in the case of Strong Verbs, the Preterit Plural), and the Past Participle. Thus,

drīfan, *to drive;*	drāf, drifon ;	drifen.
dēman, *to judge;*	dēmde ;	dēmed.

CLASSIFICATION OF STRONG VERBS.

82. One of the features of the Indo-European group of languages is the use of ablaut or vowel gradation. This permitted the construction with the same root (which could be consonants only or consonants and a vowel) of several words or forms distinguished by different vowels. Thus in Greek, the verb **lego** means *read*, and the noun **logos** means word. The principle did not permit the use of vowels at random, however. Only one qualitative ablaut and several quantitative ones were in use. The qualitative ablaut is **e, o, ē, ō,** -

(The "⁻" means that forms could be made without the vowel at all). Three principal parts of the Greek irregular verb **leipo** illustrate this ablaut: **leipo, leloipa, elipon**, in the last of which the ablaut-vowel has disappeared. The quantitative ablauts are a, ā; o, ō, etc. Though ablaut is a characteristic of Indo-European, only in Germanic was it used organically in a verbal system. In all the Germanic languages it appears as a distinguishing feature of the so-called strong verbs.[1] In accordance with the roots and ablaut used, the strong verbs are divided into seven classes.

83. (1) Class I. — In Indo-European the roots of this class had a short i; to these roots the e, o ablaut was added. Thus the stems of the principal parts had the following: ei; oi, i; i (>Germ. ei > ī; ai, i; i). Sound changes transformed these to ī; ā, i; i.

(a) **bīdan,** *bide;*   **bād, bidon;**   **biden.**
     bītan, *bite;*   **bāt, biton;**   **biten.**

     glīdan, *glide;*   **glād, glidon;**   **glidon.**
     rīdan, *ride;*   **rād, ridon;**   **riden.**
     rīsan, *rise;*   **rās, rison;**   **risen.**
     wrītan, *write;*   **wrāt, writon;**   **writen.**

(b) **sniðan,** *cut;*   **snāð, snidon;**   **sniden.**

(c) **ðēon,** *thrive;*   **ðāh, ðigon;**   **ðigen.**

---

[1] It is to be kept in mind that the principal parts of English strong verbs (e.g., *begin, began, begun*) are not irregular as some high-school grammars erroneously lead students to believe, but regularly follow a fixed system of vowel gradation.

lviii *AN OUTLINE OF ANGLO-SAXON GRAMMAR.*

(2) In **snīðan** and **ðēon** (< *ðīhan, 83, Note 3) medial **ð** and **h** of the first two parts are changed into **d** and **g** in the pret. pl. and pp. (past participle). This change from **ð** to **d**, **h** to **g**, also (in other classes of verbs) from **h** to **w** (**g**) (< hw — gw) and **s** to **r**, is called Grammatical Change (S. §§ 233–234).

NOTE 1. — Grammatical Change (only partly preserved) is due to an original (pre-Germanic) difference of accent, according to which the pret. pl. and the pp. were accented on the final syllable (Verner's Law).

NOTE 2. — The weak verb **rignan** > **rīnan** (16), *to rain*, pret. **rinde**, has also a preterit **rān** (cf. **frignan** > **frīnan**, 85, Note 3).

(3) To the contract verb **ðēon** are to be added **lēon**, *to lend;* **sēon**, *to strain, sift;* **tēon**, *to censure;* **wrēon**, *to cover*. The accidental agreement in the present between these verbs and the contract verbs of Class II has resulted in the production of double forms in the other tenses. Thus,

tēon;	tāh (tēah),	tigon (tugon);	tigen (togen).
ðēon;	ðāh,	ðigon (ðugon);	ðigen (ðogen).
wrēon;	wrāh (wrēah),	wrigon (wrugon);	wrigen (wrogen).

NOTE 3. — **ðēon** has also forms according to Class III, such as pret. pl. **ofer-ðungon**; pp. **ofer-ðungen**; pp. (adj.) **ge-ðungen**, *grown, excellent*, **hēah-ðungen**, *highly prosperous*, etc. In fact the verb belonged originally to the third class, but regular sound changes converted the present and singular preterit into forms that had no similarity to forms of that class: *ðenhan > *ðinhan (6) > *ðīhan (8, Note) > *ðīohan (10 (b)) > ðīon or ðēon (18, Note 2); *ðanh > *ðōh (8, Note) or possibly ðāh. No sound changes, however, affected **ðungon**, **ðungen**.

84. Class II. — Original verbs had **u** in the stem; to this was added the same ablaut as in Class I, producing **eu; ou, u; u** (> Germ. **eu; au, u; u**). In Anglo-Saxon these became **ēo; ēa, u; o**. A few verbs have **ū** in the present.

INFLECTION: CONJUGATION. lix

(a) bēodan, *command;* bēad, budon; boden.
    clēofan, *cleave;* clēaf, clufon; clofen.
    crēopan, *creep;* crēap, crupon; cropen.
    drēogan, *endure;* drēag, drugon; drogen.
    flēogan, *fly;* flēag, flugon; flogen.

(b) brūcan, *enjoy;* brēac, brucon; brocen.
    būgan, *bow;* bēag, bugon; bogen.
    dūfan, *dive;* dēaf, dufon; dofen.

(c) cēosan, *choose;* cēas, curon (83, 2); coren.
    frēosan, *freeze;* frēas, fruron; froren.
    hrēosan, *fall;* hrēas, hruron; hroren.
    (for)lēosan, *lose;* lēas, luron; loren.
    sēoðan, *seethe;* sēað, sudon; soden.

(d) flēon (18, N.2), *flee;* flēah, flugon; flogen.
    tēon, *draw;* tēah, tugon; togen.

85. Class III. — Originally this class used the same ablaut as Classes I and II: e; o, -; - (>Germ. e; a (13, *d*, Note), u; u. In the last two principal parts, where the ablaut did not appear, a u later was developed), followed immediately by a consonant group. The verbs of this class are best considered in four divisions.

(1) Verbs with a nasal + consonant after the radical vowel. Thus,

bindan (6), *bind;* bǫnd (8), bundon; { bunden (13, *d*, Note).
drincan, *drink;* drǫnc, druncon; druncen.
findan, *find;* fǫnd, fundon; funden.
(on)ginnan, *begin;* gǫn(n), gunnon; gunnen.
grindan, *grind;* grǫnd, grundon; grunden.
singan, *sing;* sǫng, sungon; sungen.
swimman, *swim;* swǫm(m), swummon; swummen.

NOTE 1. — The verb rinnan, *to run*, rǫn(n), runnon, runnen, is more commonly used with metathesis in the first two parts: irnan (iernan, yrnan), ǫrn (arn). — There is also metathesis in beornan (= Goth. brinnan), *to burn*, brǫn(n) (bǫrn, barn, bearn), burnon, burnen.

lx AN OUTLINE OF ANGLO-SAXON GRAMMAR.

(2) Verbs with l + consonant after the radical vowel. Thus,

(a) helpan (10, a, 2), help; { healp / (10, a, 1) }, hulpon; { holpen / (13, d, Note) }.
    belgan, be angry;   bealg, bulgon; bolgen.
    delfan, delve;   dealf, dulfon; dolfen.
    meltan, melt;   mealt, multon; molten.
    swelgan, swallow; swealg, swulgon; swolgen.
    swellan, swell; sweal(l), swullon; swollen.
    sweltan, die; swealt, swulton; swolten.

(b) gieldan (11, c), yield; geald, guldon; golden.
    giellan, yell; geal(l), gullon; gollen.
    gielpan, boast; gealp, gulpon; golpen.

(c) fēolan, (17) reach; fealh, fulgon (83, 2); folgen.

NOTE 2. — fēolan < *feolhan (10, a, 2) (= Goth. filhan); there is also a pret. pl. fǣlon and a pp. folen according to Class IV.

(3) Verbs with r + consonant after the radical vowel. Thus,

(a) beorgan / (10, a, 2) }, protect; bearg, burgon; { borgen / (13, d, Note) }.
    ceorfan, carve; cearf, curfon; corfen.
    deorfan, labor; dearf, durfon; dorfen.
    smeortan, smart; smeart, smurton; smorten.

(b) hweorfan / (hwurfan, 19) }, turn; hwearf, hwurfon; hworfen.
    weorpan / (wurpan) }, cast; wearp, wurpon; worpen.

(c) weorðan / (wurðan, 19) }, become; wearð, { wurdon / (83, 2) }; worden.

(4) Certain remaining verbs of this class are best considered together.

  feohtan (10, a, 2), fight; { feaht / (10, a, 1) } { fuhton; fohten.
  bregdan / (brēdan, 16) }, brandish; { brægd / (brǣd) }, { brugdon / (brūdon); } { brogden / (brōden).
  stregdan / (strēdan) }, strew; { strægd / (strǣd) }, { strugdon / (strūdon); } { strogden / (strōden).

INFLECTION: CONJUGATION. lxi

berstan, *burst*;	bærst,	burston;	borsten.
ðerscan, *thresh*;	ðærsc,	ðurscon;	ðorscen.
frignan (frīnan, 16) }, *inquire*;	{ frægn (frān),	{ frugnon (frūnon);	{ frugnen (frūnen).
murnan, *mourn*;	mearn,	murnon.	
spurnan (spornan) }, *spurn*;	spearn,	spurnon.	

NOTE 3. — stregdan has also become a weak verb. — By the loss of g and the compensatory lengthening of the radical vowel frignan becomes frīnan (16), and being thus attracted to Class I, yields the preterit frān. There is also occasionally assimilation of g to n resulting in frinnan, pret. pl. frunnon, etc. The metathesis of n appears in pret. sg. freng, pret. pl. frungon. Other forms are: pret. pl. frugon; pp. gefrugen, gefregen, gefrægen and gefrigen (cf. 87, Note).

86. Class IV. — This class used the ablaut series e; o, ē; - (> Germ. e (i) (6); a, ē; u), followed by a single liquid or nasal. The vowels in Anglo-Saxon became e (i); æ, ǣ; o (u) (13, *d*).

(*a*) beran, *bear*;   bær (9),   bǣron;   boren.
    cwelan, *die*;   cwæl,   cwǣlon;   cwolen.
    helan, *conceal*;   hæl,   hǣlon;   holen.
    stelan, *steal*;   stæl,   stǣlon;   stolen.
    teran, *tear*;   tær,   tǣron;   toren.

(*b*) brecan, *break*;   bræc,   brǣcon;   brocen.

(*c*) scieran (11. *c*), *shear*; scear, scēaron; scoren.

(*d*) niman, *take*;   { nōm (nam), | { nōmon (nāmon); | numen. { cumen (cymen). |
    cuman, *come*;   c(w)ōm,   c(w)ōmon;

NOTE. — In brecan the r precedes the radical vowel; it should therefore be found in Class V (cf. sprecan). — niman has changed e to i before m, and the u of cuman is exceptional. The Germanic infinitive of cuman was cweman. The Anglo-Saxon infinitive comes from a stem in which the ablaut disappeared and the w vocalized to u. The preterits of these two verbs are also exceptional in having ō (< ǣ before a nasal) in the pl., which has also been transferred into the sing. The LWS forms are usually nam, nāmon, cōm, cōmon.

AN OUTLINE OF ANGLO-SAXON GRAMMAR.

87. Class V. — This class of verbs differs from Class IV (1) in having the ablaut series followed by a single consonant, not a liquid or nasal, and (2) in having e in the past participle: e; o, ē; e (< Germ. e; a (13, *d*), ē; e). These vowels became in Anglo-Saxon e; æ, ǣ; e. Thus,

(*a*) metan, *measure;*   mæt(9), mǣton;   meten.
   drepan, *strike;*   dræp, drǣpon;   { drepen (dropen).
   lesan, *collect;*   læs, lǣson;   lesen.
   (ge)nesan, *recover;*   næs, nǣson;   nesen.
   { sprecan, *speak;*   spræc, sprǣcon;   sprecen.
   { specan (LWS);   spæc, spǣcon;   specen.
   tredan, *tread;*   træd, trǣdon;   treden.
   wegan, *carry;*   wæg, { wǣgon (wāgon);   wegen.

(*b*) etan, *eat;*   ǣt, ǣton;   eten.
   fretan, *devour;*   frǣt, frǣton;   freten.

(*c*) cweðan, *say;*   cwæð, cwǣdon(83, 2); cweden.

(*d*) giefan (11, *c*), *give;*   geaf, gēafon;   giefen.
   gietan, *get;*   geat, gēaton;   gieten.

(*e*) (ge)fēon 18, N. 2) }, *rejoice;* { gefeah (10, *a*, 1), gefǣgon (83,2); (adj.) gefægen.
   plēon, *risk;*   pleah.
   sēon, *see;*   seah, { sāwon (83, 2); { sewen (sawen) sǣgon;   segen.

(*f*) Several presents are formed in **-jan**. In Germanic the radical vowel e, when thus followed by **-j**, became **i**; and the final radical consonant is geminated (7). Thus,

biddan (= Goth. bidjan), *bid;* } bæd, bǣdon;   beden.
licg(e)an, *lie;*   læg, lǣgon (lāgon); legen.
sittan, *sit;*   sæt sǣton;   seten.
fricg(e)an, *inquire;*   frigen.
ðicg(e)an, *take;*   ðeah (ðāh).

INFLECTION: CONJUGATION. lxiii

NOTE. — The quantity of ǣt and frǣt is exceptional. — Verbs in g may have ā in the pret. pl. (lāgon, wāgon). — fricg(e)an does not occur in the pret. The pp. frigen may belong to frignan (cf. 85, Note 3). — ðicg(e)an has also weak preterits ðigede and ðigde.

88. Class VI. — The Indo-European quantitative ablauts a, ā; o, ō fell together in Germanic since ā regularly became ō, and o became a. Thus the Germanic (and Anglo-Saxon) ablaut a; ō, ō; a resulted.

(a) faran, *go;*   fōr,   fōron;   faren (færen).
    bacan, *bake;*   bōc,   bōcon;   bacen.
    dragan, *draw;*   drōg,   drōgon;   dragen.
    galan, *sing;*   gōl,   gōlon;   galen.
    grafan, *grave;*   grōf,   grōfon;   grafen.
    hladan, *load;*   hlōd,   hlōdon;   hladen.
    sacan, *contend;*   sōc,   sōcon;   sacen (sæcen).
    stǫndan, *stand;*   stōd,   stōdon;   stǫnden.
    wadan, *go;*   wōd,   wōdon;   waden.
    [wæcnan], *awake;*   wōc,   wōcon.

(b) sc(e)acan ⎫ *shake,*   ⎧ scōc,   scōcon.   ⎧ sc(e)acen
    (11, N. 1) ⎭ *hasten;* ⎨   ⎨ (scæcen).
                           ⎩ scēoc,   scēocon;   ⎩
    sc(e)afan, *shave;*   scōf,   scōfon;   sc(e)afen.

(c) spǫnan, *entice;*   ⎧ spōn   ⎧ spōnon
                         ⎩ (spēon),   ⎩ (spēonon);   spanen.

    weaxan   ⎫ *grow;*   (wōx)   ⎧ (wōxon)   weaxen.
    (10, a, 1) ⎭   wēox,   ⎩ wēoxon;

(d) flēan (18, N. 2), *flay;* flōg (flōh), flōgon;   flagen.
    lēan, *blame;*   lōg (lōh),   lōgon;   ⎧ lagen (lęgen,
                                                             ⎩ lægen).
    slēan, *strike;*   slōg (slōh), slōgon;   ⎧ slagen, slęgen,
                                                             ⎩ slægen).
                               ⎧ ðwōg   ⎧ ðwagen
    ðwēan, *wash;*   ⎨   ðwōgon;   ⎪ (ðwęgen,
                               ⎩ (ðwōh),   ⎨ ðwægen,
                                                              ⎩ ðwogen).

(e) Presents in -jan (cf. 87, *f*):

    hębban (7), *heave;*   hōf,   hōfon;   hafen (hæfen).
    hliehhan, *laugh;*   hlōh,   hlōgon (83, 2).
    ⎧ scęððan, *injure;*   scōd,   scōdon.
    ⎩ sceaððan (11, N.1); scēod, scēodon.

lxiv AN OUTLINE OF ANGLO-SAXON GRAMMAR.

scieppan (7), *create*;	{ scōp, scēop (11, N. 1),	scōpon ; scēopon ;	{ scępen (sceapen).
stęppan (stæppan) }, *step*;		stōp,	stōpon ; stapen.
swęri(ge)an (11, N. 3) }, *swear*;		swōr,	swōron ; { swaren (sworen).

NOTE 1. — In the pp. the vowel **a** is often changed to **ę** or **æ**. — **wæcnan** is a weak present, which, in the absence of a strong form, is associated with the pret. **wōc**. — **spǫnan** (LWS also **spǫnnan**) has the additional pret. **spēon**, which is due to association with Class VII verbs (cf. **spǫnnan**, *to span*). — **weaxan** (**weahsan**) has adopted commonly the pret. of a Class VII verb.

NOTE 2. — In **flōg, lōg, slōg**, etc. (for **flōh**, etc.), grammatical change (**83**, 2) has yielded to the influence of the pl. ; the return to **flōh**, etc., is due to the change of final **g** to **h** (**16**, Note).

NOTE 3. — Some of these verbs have also weak forms: **hębban**, pret. **hęfde**, pp. **hęfod** ; **scęðð̵an**, pret. **scęð̵ede** ; **swęrian**, **swęrede**, etc.

89. Class VII. — (1) There is less genetic unity in this class than in any of the preceding. In fact it is composed of several kinds of stems, a variety of ablauts, has many analogical forms altered by influence of other forms, and has a few peculiar forms perhaps derived from reduplicated originals. These last were made by prefixing to the stem a syllable composed of the first consonant of the stem + **e**. Such forms are found in Gothic (as well as Latin and Greek), and they may underlie such peculiar preterits in Anglo-Saxon as **heht**, from **hātan** ; **leolc**, from **lācan** ; **leort**, from **lǣtan** ; **reord** from **rǣdan**, and **ondreord** from **ondrǣdan**. In the main, however, the verbs of Class VII are based on ablauts.

(2) Verbs of Class VII have the same radical vowel in the entire preterit ; and the radical vowel of the past participle is the same as that of the present.

INFLECTION: CONJUGATION. lxv

90. Verbs of Class VII form two classes : (1) the ē-preterit class, and (2) the ēo-preterit class. The radical vowels of the present are regarded in subdivisions of these classes.

(1) ē-Preterit Class.

(a) blǫndan (8), *blend;*	blēnd,	blēndon ;	blǫnden.
(b) hātan, *call;*	heht, hēt,	hēton ;	hāten.
lācan, *leap;*	(leolc) lēc,	lēcon ;	lācen.
{ scādan, *separate,*	scēd,	scēdon ;	scāden.
{ scēadan (11, N. 1);	scēad,	scēadon ;	scēaden.

NOTE 1. — The verb **hātan** has other forms of special importance : (1c) **hātte**, *I am called* (*named*, '*hight*') is the sole relic of a mediopassive conjugation, and corresponds to Goth. **haitada** ; the corresponding pl. **hātton** has the common weak pret. form. As to tense **hātte, hātton** are used both as presents and as preterits, and the infinitive **hātan** is also used with this passive sense.

(c) (on)drǣdan, *fear;*	{ (dreord) drēd,	drēdon ;	drǣden.
lǣtan, *let;*	(leort) lēt,	lēton ;	lǣten.
rǣdan, *council;*	(reord) rēd,	rēdon ;	rǣden.
slǣpan (slāpan) }, *sleep;*	slēp,	slēpon ;	{ slǣpen. (slāpen).

NOTE 2. — (on)**drǣdan** and **slǣpan** occasionally have the pret. weak : **ondrǣdde, slēpte, slāpte,** etc. — **rǣdan**, on the other hand, is commonly conjugated as a weak verb : pret. **rǣdde.**

(d) fōn (18, N. 2), *seize;*	fēng,	fēngon ;	fǫngen.
hōn, *hang;*	hēng,	hēngon ;	hǫngen.

(2) ēo-Preterit Class.

(a) fealdan (10, a, 1), *fold;*	fēold,	fēoldon ;	fealden.
feallan, *fall;*	fēoll,	fēollon ;	feallen.
healdan, *hold;*	hēold,	hēoldon ;	healden.
wealcan, *roll;*	wēolc,	wēolcon ;	wealcen.
wealdan, *wield;*	wēold,	wēoldon ;	wealden.
weallan, *well;*	wēoll,	wēollon ;	weallen.
weaxan, (88, N. 1) }, *grow;*	wēox,	wēoxon ;	weaxen.

(b) bǫnnan, *summon;* (bēnn) bēonn, -on; bǫnnen.
    spǫnnan, *attack;* (spēnn) spēonn, -on; spǫnnen.
    gǫngan, *go;* (gēng) gēong, -on; gǫngen.

NOTE 3. — gǫngan is very irregular; there is an inf. **gengan**, pret. **gēng** and **gēngde**; also **gang**. The most commonly used pret. **ēode** belongs to **gān (107, 4)**.

(c) bēatan, *beat;* bēot, bēoton; bēaten.
    hēawan, *hew;* hēow, hēowon; hēawen.
    hlēapan, *leap;* hlēop, hlēopon; hlēapen.
    (ā)hnēapan, *pluck;* hnēop, hnēopon; hnēapen

(d) blōtan, *sacrifice;* blēot, blēoton; blōten.
    hrōpan, *shout;* hrēop, hrēopon; hrōpen.
    hwōpan, *threaten;* hwēop, hwēopon; hwōpen.
    blōwan, *bloom;* blēow, blēowon; blōwen.
    flōwan, *flow;* flēow, flēowon; flōwen.
    grōwan, *grow;* grēow, grēowon; grōwen.
    rōwan, *row;* rēow, rēowon; rōwen.
    spōwan, *succeed;* spēow, spēowon; spōwen.

(e) **jan**-presents (cf. 87, *f*):

    hwēsan, *wheeze;* hwēos, hwēoson; hwōsen.
    wēpan, *weep;* wēop, wēopon; wōpen.

(f) blāwan, *blow,* blēow, blēowon; blāwen.
    cnāwan, *know;* cnēow, cnēowon; cnāwen.
    crāwan, *crow;* crēow, crēowon; crāwen.
    sāwan, *sow;* sēow, sēowon; sāwen.
    swāpan, *sweep;* swēop, swēopon; swāpen.

INFLECTION: CONJUGATION. lxvii

CONJUGATION OF STRONG VERBS. (S. §§ 350-378.)

91. Themes: Ablaut verbs, **singan**, *to sing;* **beran**, *to bear;* **healdan**, *to hold.*

PRESENT.

Indicative.

Sing. 1.	singe	bere	healde
2.	singest	bir(e)st	hieltst, healdest
3.	singeð	bir(e)ð	hielt, healt, healdeð
Plur. 1-3.	singað	berað	healdað

Optative.

Sing. 1-3.	singe	bere	healde
Plur. 1-3.	singen	beren	healden

Imperative.

Sing. 2.	sing	ber	heald
Plur. 2.	singað	berað	healdað

Infinitive.	singan	beran	healdan
Gerund.	{ tō singanne (-enne, -onne) }	beranne	healdanne
Pres. Part.	singende	berende	healdende

PRETERIT.

Indicative.

Sing. 1.	sǫng	bær	hēold
2.	sunge	bǣre	hēolde
3.	sǫng	bær	hēold
Plur. 1-3.	sungon	bǣron	hēoldon

Optative.

Sing. 1-3.	sunge	bǣre	hēolde
Plur. 1-3.	sungen	bǣren	hēolden

Past Part.	(ge)sungen	(ge)boren	(ge)healden

92. Themes: Contracted presents (**18,** Note 2), **sēon,** *to see;* **fōn,** *to seize.* — Presents in -jan, **biddan,** *to bid;* **licgan,** *to lie.*

PRESENT.

Indicative.

Sing. 1.	sēo	fō	bidde	licge
2.	siehst	fēhst	{bid(e)st / bitst}	lig(e)st
3.	siehð	fēhð	{bideð / bit(t)}	{lig(e)ð / lið}
Plur. 1–3.	sēoð	fōð	biddað	licgað

Optative.

Sing. 1–3.	sēo	fō	bidde	licge
Plur. 1–3.	sēon	fōn	bidden	licgen

Imperative.

Sing. 2.	seoh	fōh	bide	lige
Plur. 2.	sēoð	fōð	biddað	licgað

Infinitive.	sēon	fōn	biddan	licgan
Gerund.	tō sēonne	fōnne	biddanne	licganne
Pres. Part.	sēonde	fōnde	biddende	licgende

PRETERIT.

Indicative.

Sing. 1.	seah	fēng	bæd	læg
2.	sāwe	fēnge	bǣde	lǣge
3.	seah	fēng	bæd	læg
Plur. 1–3.	sāwon	fēngon	bǣdon	lǣgon

Optative.

Sing. 1–3.	sāwe	fēnge	bǣde	lǣge
Plur. 1–3.	sāwen	fēngen	bǣden	lǣgen

Past Part.	(ge)sewen	(ge)fongen	(ge)beden	(ge)legen

INFLECTION: CONJUGATION. lxix

93. (1) The personal endings of the verb exhibit some variations. The older ending of the 1 sg. pres. indic. is **-u** (**-o**), but its use is restricted even in EWS; the prevailing ending is **-e** (conforming to **-est, -eð**).

The 2 sg. pres. indic. originally ended in **-es** (< *-is); the subjoined pronoun ðū contributed the added t. In EWS **-es** is occasionally found, and sometimes the intermediate form **-esð**, but the common form is **-est**.

The older ending of the pret. indic. pl. **-un** is used in EWS, but not as frequently as **-on** (**-an**). In LWS the regular ending **-on** is often weakened to **-an, -un**, etc.

For the opt. pl. ending **-en**, pres. and pret., **-on** and **-an** sometimes occur in EWS; but in LWS this ending **-en** is very commonly disguised under the weakened forms **-on, -an, -un**, etc.

(2) When the pronominal subjects **wē**, *we*, **gē**, *ye*, are placed immediately after the verb, the verbal ending is often (not uniformly) reduced to **-e**. Originally this form was in all probability restricted to the adhortative optative; the **-e** would therefore represent a reduction of **-en**. But in the historic periods of West-Saxon the indic. pres. and pret. and the imperative (**-að** and **-on** also giving way to **-e**) are found attracted into this usage.

Thus, **wē (gē) cweðað**, but **cweðe wē (gē); wē (gē) magon**, but **mage wē (gē); wē (gē) nimen**, but **nime wē (gē); wē (gē) cōmon (sōhton)**, but **cōme (sōhte) wē (gē)**.

(3) The 2 sg. imperative of presents in **-jan** with short radical vowel has the ending **-e**, and is without gemination of the radical consonant (**bide, lige**).

NOTE. — The 2 sg. pret. of ablaut verbs has that form of the radical vowel which belongs to the pret. pl. and optative; it is, presumably, an optative form transferred into the indicative (cf. **105**, 2).

(4) The 2 and 3 sg. pres. indic. have three special features: (1) the radical consonant of presents in jan is not geminated (bidest, bideð; ligest, ligeð) because the older endings contain no -j- (*-is, *-ið). But in all other present forms (except 2 sg. imperative), since a -j- was present in the endings, gemination occurred. (2) In the second and third singular the radical vowel is umlauted if it is susceptible to umlaut. Likewise e became i (87 (f)). (3) The personal endings may be syncopated, that is, the e of -est, -eð may disappear; the consequent combination of the final radical consonant and -st, -ð produces results the more common of which are the following:

(a) d + st becomes tst: biddan, ðū bitst; stondan, ðū stentst. This coincides with t + st: bītan, ðū bītst; gietan, ðū gi(e)tst.

(b) ð + st becomes tst or st: snīðan, ðū snītst; weorðan, ðū wi(e)rst; cweðan, ðū cwist.

(c) g + st becomes (less frequently) hst: lēogan, ðū lī(e)hst; stīgan, ðū stīgst, stīhst. And occasionally c + st becomes hst: sēcan, ðū sēcst, sēhst; but brūcan, ðū brȳcst, etc.

(d) d and t + ð become t or tt: biddan, hē bidt, bit(t); bebēodan, hē bebīet(t); etan, hē it(t); feohtan, hē fieht; hātan, hē hǣt.

(e) ð + ð becomes ð: cweðan, hē cwið: snīðan, hē snīð; weorðan, hē wierð.

(f) s + ð becomes st: cēosan, hē cīest; gehrēosan, hē gehrī(e)st; forlēosan, hē forlī(e)st.

(g) g + ð becomes (less frequently) hð: drēogan, hē drī(e)gð, drī(e)hð; lēogan, hē lī(e)gð, lī(e)hð. Occasionally c + ð becomes hð: sēcan, hē sēcð, sēhð; but ðyncan, ðyncð, etc.

INFLECTION: CONJUGATION. lxxi

CLASSIFICATION OF WEAK VERBS. (S. § 398.)

94. There are three classes of Weak Verbs: (1) the ja-class, (2) the ō-class, and (3) the ai-class. The Preterit and the Past Participle of all classes are formed in d (t).

NOTE 1. — The formative and derivative -ja- (more strictly, -eja-) is the same element which is employed in the presents of strong verbs in -jan. The verbs of the First Class may, therefore, with equal propriety, be called verbs in -jan.

NOTE 2. — Most weak verbs are derivative. Thus, dōm, *judgment*, > dēman (< *dōmian), *to judge;* cūð, adj., *known,* > cȳðan (< *cūðian), *to make known;* feorr, adv., *far,* > ā-fierran (< *-feorrian), *to remove;* tāc(e)n, *token,* > tācnian (< *tācnōjan), *to betoken*.

Some weak verbs are the transitive (or causative) complements of corresponding intransitive strong verbs, the radical syllable of the weak verb corresponding to that of the pret. sg. of the strong verb. Thus, licgan, *to lie,* pret. sg. læg, — lęcgan, *to lay* (< *lægjan); sittan, *to sit,* pret. sg. sæt, — sęttan, *to set* (< *sætjan); cwelan, *to die,* pret. sg. cwæl, — cwęllan, *to kill* (< *cwæljan); rīsan, *to rise,* pret. sg. rās, — rǣran, *to rear, raise* (< *rārian; r < s); drincan, *to drink,* pret. sg. drǫnc, — dręncan, *to drench* (< *drǫncian).

CONJUGATION OF THE FIRST CLASS OF WEAK VERBS.
(S. §§ 409, 410.)

95. Themes: fręmman, *to perform;* hęrian, *to praise.* dēman, *to judge;* lǣdan, *to lead.*

PRESENT.

Indicative.

Sing. 1.	fręmme	hęrie	dēme	lǣde
2.	fręmest	hęrest	dēm(e)st	{ lǣd(e)st / lǣtst
3.	fręmeð	hęreð	dēm(e)ð	{ lǣdeð, lǣdt, / lǣt
Plur. 1–3.	fręmmað	hęriað	dēmað	lǣdað

AN OUTLINE OF ANGLO-SAXON GRAMMAR.

Optative.

Sing. 1–3.	fremme	herie	dēme	lǣde
Plur. 1–3.	fremmen	herien	dēmen	lǣden

Imperative.

Sing. 2.	freme	here	dēm	lǣd
Plur. 2.	fremmaðˀ	heriaðˀ	dēmaðˀ	lǣdaðˀ

Infinitive.	fremman	herian	dēman	lǣdan
Gerund.	{ tō fremmanne (-enne, -onne)	herianne	dēmanne	lǣdanne
Pres. Part.	fremmende	heriende	dēmende	lǣdende

PRETERIT.

Indicative.

Sing. 1.	fremede	herede	dēmde	lǣdde
2.	fremedest	heredest	dēmdest	lǣddest
3.	fremede	herede	dēmde	lǣdde
Plur. 1–3.	fremedon	heredon	dēmdon	lǣddon

Optative.

Sing. 1–3.	fremede	herede	dēmde	lǣdde
Plur. 1–3.	fremeden	hereden	dēmden	lǣdden

Past Part.	(ge)fremed	(ge)hered	(ge)dēmed	{ (ge)lǣded ((ge)lǣd(d)

96. (1) The **j** (**i**) of the element **-ja** (which became -ia- after a long radical syllable; cf. **7**, Note 2) produces umlaut of the radical vowel, and gemination of the final radical consonant, when single (except **r**), after a short radical vowel (**7**).

Thus, **fremman** (< *fremjan); **herian** (< *hærjan); **dēman** (< *dōmian).

(2) The radical consonant is not geminated in the 2 and 3 sg. pres. indic., and in the 2 sg. imperative (cf. **93**, 3, 4): **fremest, fremeðˀ, freme**.

INFLECTION: CONJUGATION. lxxiii

Verbs in **r** exhibit the various graphic substitutions for **i** (**j**) + a vowel (**11**, Note 3). Thus, **hęrian, hęrgan, hęrigean**, etc.; 1 sg. pres. indic. **hęrie, hęrge, herige**, etc.

NOTE 1. — In the 2 and 3 sg. pres. indic. syncope of the vowel of the personal ending is most frequent with verbs having a long radical syllable: **dēm(e)st, dēm(e)ð**, etc.

(**3**) The 2 sg. imperative ends in **-e** (without gemination of the radical consonant), but when the radical syllable is long this ending disappears: **fręme, dēm** (cf. **93**, 3).

NOTE 2. — In a few instances in EWS and somewhat oftener in LWS, the 2 sg. imperative ending -e is found after a long adical syllable: **lǣre**, *teach;* **sęnde**, *send;* **hiere**, *hear*

(**4**) An external agreement in some forms between verbs in **r** (like **hęrian**; **nęrian**, *to save;* **dęrian**, *to injure*) and verbs of the Second Class, has gradually brought these verbs in **r** into more or less frequent and complete conformity with the conjugation of the Second Class. Thus, 3 sg. pres. indic. **dęreð** and **dęrað**; pret. sg. **nęrede** and **nęrode**; **styrian**, *to stir*, pret. sg. **styrede** and **styrode**.

This resultant double mode of conjugation has also been extended to other verbs. Thus, **fręmman** and **fręmian**, 3 sg. pres. indic. **fręmeð** and **fręmað**, pret. sg. **fręmede** and **fręmode**, pp. **fręmed** and **fręmod**; **dwęllan** (**98**) and **dwęlian**, *to deceive;* **trymman** and **trymian**, *to confirm*, etc.

lxxiv *AN OUTLINE OF ANGLO-SAXON GRAMMAR.*

FORMATION OF THE PRETERIT TENSE AND OF THE PAST PARTICIPLE. (S. §§ 401-408.)

97. (1) Verbs with an originally short radical syllable (i.e. those which admit of gemination of the final radical consonant and those in r; 7) have the pret. (sg.) in -ede and the pp. in -ed, without gemination of the radical consonant and with umlaut of the radical vowel: fremede, (ge)fremed; herede, (ge)hered.

NOTE. — lecgan, *to lay*, is exceptional in having syncope of the middle vowel: pret. legde (lēde, 16), pp. legd (lēd).

NOTE 2. — Verbs in d or t syncopate the middle vowel and t + d becomes tt: hreddan, *to liberate*, pret. hredde, pp. hred(d); treddan, *to tread*, pret. tredde, pp. tred(d); lettan, *to hinder*, pret. lette, pp. let(t); settan, *to set*, pret. sette, pp. set(t). In the uninflected form these participles sometimes retain the middle vowel: treded, seted, etc.

So also verbs in the derivative -ettan (= -ettan; Goth. -atjan), like bliccettan, *to lighten*, ondettan, *to confess*, ōnettan, *to hasten*, hālettan, *to salute*, and licettan, *to pretend*, pret. licette, pp. licet(t).

(2) Verbs with an originally long radical syllable syncopate the middle vowel in the preterit (-ede > -de), and usually in the inflected forms of the past participle that have a vocalic case-ending. The radical vowel is umlauted: pret. dēmde, pp. dēmed, pl. dēmde.

NOTE 3. — The pp. of verbs in d or t (cf. **97**, Note 2) often syncopate the middle vowel: lǣded, lǣd(d); hȳdan, *to hide*, pret. hȳdde, pp. hȳded, hȳd(d); mētan, *to meet*, pret. mētte, pp. mēted, mēt(t).

When preceded by a consonant, d + d and tt (< t + d) are simplified: sendan, *to send*, pret. sende, pp. sended, send; wendan, *to turn*, pret. wende, pp. wended, wend; hæftan, *to seize*, pret. hæfte, pp. hæfted, hæft; wēstan, *to lay waste*, pret. wēste, pp. wēsted, wēst.

NOTE 4. — Other phonetic changes resulting from the combination of a final radical consonant and the d of the pret. and pp. are the following:

(*a*) After a voiceless consonant (c, p, t, ff, ss, x (= cs)), d becomes t: drencan, *to drench*, pret. drencte, pp. drenced, pl. drencte; hys-

INFLECTION: CONJUGATION. lxxv

pan, *to revile*, pret. hyspte; clyppan, *to embrace*, pret. clypte, pp. clypt; for verbs in t see the preceding Note; cyssan, *to kiss*, pret. cyste, pp. cyssed; lixan, *to shine*, pret. lixte.

Verbs in the derivative -lǣc(e)an have the pret. and pp. in ct or ht: nēalǣcan, *to approach*, pret. nēalǣcte, nēalǣhte, pp. nēalǣct, nēalǣht. This change of ct into ht is found occasionally in other verbs: īecan, *to increase*, pret. īecte, īehte, pp. īeced, iect, īeht; ðryccan, *to oppress*, pret. ðrycte, ðryhte, pp. ðrycced.

(*b*) ð + d remains, or becomes dd: cȳðan, *to make known*, pret. cȳðde, cȳdde, pp. cȳðed, cȳd(d); nēðan, *to venture*, pret. nēðde, nēdde.

(*c*) The usual pret. of nęmnan, *to name*, is nęmde, and of ęfnan, ræfnan, *to perform*, ęfnde, ræfnde; but verbs in a consonant + n, l, r generally retain the n, l, or r in the form of a syllable (ne; el, le; er, re), and are thus attracted, particularly in LWS, into the Second Conjugation: pret. nęmnode, ęfnede; pp. nęmned, nęmnod, pl. nęmde, nęmnede, nęmnode; timbran (timbrian), *to build*, pret. timberde, timbrede, timbrode, pp. timbred, timbrod; dieglan, *to conceal*, pret. dīegelde, dīeglede, dīeglode, etc.

(*d*) In the pret. and pp. of verbs in rw and lw the w sometimes disappears: gierwan, *to prepare*, pret. gierede, pp. gierwed, giered; wielwan, *to roll*, pret. wielede, pp. wielwed. Many of these verbs (with or without the w in all forms) are attracted in LWS into the Second Conjugation: smierwan, *to anoint*, smyrian; pret. smyrode, pp. smyrod; wielwan (wylwian, wyllan).

VERBS WITHOUT THE MIDDLE VOWEL. (S. § 407.)

98. The verbs of the following group form the preterit and past participle without the middle vowel e (<i). These verbs have therefore two special features: (1) The lack of umlaut in the preterit and past participle; and (2) the (Germanic) change of original c and g+d into ht.

Thus, cwęcc(e)an (11, Note 2), *to shake*, < *cwæcjan (7), pret. cweahte < *cwæhte (10, *a*, 1); sēc(e)an, *to seek*, < *sōcian, pret. sōhte; ðęnc(e)an, *to think*, < *ðǫncian (8), pret. ðōhte < *ðǫnhte; ðync(e)an, *to seem*, pret. ðūhte < *ðunhte.

AN OUTLINE OF ANGLO-SAXON GRAMMAR.

NOTE 1. — ðōhte and ðūhte illustrate the Germanic disappearance of n before the voiceless spirant h, with compensatory lengthening of the preceding vowel (cf. 8, Note).

The group is as follows:

cwęllan, *kill;*	cwealde;	cweald.
dwęllan, *deceive;*	dwealde;	dweald.
sęllan, *give;*	sealde;	seald.
stęllan, *place;*	stealde;	steald.
tęllan, *count;*	tealde;	teald.
cwęcc(e)an, *shake;*	{ cweahte; { cwęhte;	cweaht. cwęht.
dręcc(e)an, *vex;*	dreahte, (ę);	dreaht, (ę).
lęcc(e)an, *moisten;*	leahte, (ę);	leaht, (ę).
ręcc(e)an, *expound;*	reahte, (ę);	reaht, (ę).
stręcc(e)an, *stretch;*	streahte, (ę);	streaht, (ę).
ðęcc(e)an, *cover;*	ðeahte, (ę);	ðeaht, (ę).
węcc(e)an, *wake;*	weahte, (ę);	weaht, (ę).
læcc(e)an, *seize;*	lǣhte;	lǣht.
bepǣc(e)an, *deceive;*	bepǣhte;	pǣht.
rǣc(e)an, *reach;*	rǣhte;	rǣht.
tǣc(e)an, *teach;*	tǣhte;	tǣht.
rēc(e)an ręcc(e)an } , *reck;*	rōhte.	
sēc(e)an, *seek;*	sōhte;	sōht.
ðęnc(e)an, *think;*	ðōhte;	ðōht.
ðync(e)an, *seem;*	ðūhte;	ðūht.
wyrc(e)an, *work;*	worhte;	worht.
bycg(e)an, *buy;*	bohte;	boht.
bringan bręngan } , *bring;*	brōhte;	gebrōht.

NOTE 2. — In LWS dwęllan has also the forms dwęlian, pret. dwęlede, dwęlode, pp. dwęled, dwęlod (96. 4). A trace of an ablaut verb dwelan is found in the pret. d(w)æl. The pp. of tęllan also appears as tęled, and sęllan is in LWS usually syllan.

NOTE 3. — In LWS węcc(e)an often becomes wręcc(e)an. A difference of origin, apparently, underlies rēc(e)an (< *rōcian) and ręcc(e)an (< *ræcjan); so, too, bringan and bręngan. A trace of an ablaut verb is the pp. brungen.

NOTE 4. — In bepǣc(e)an, rǣc(e)an, and tǣc(e)an the umlauted vowel of the present has been transferred to the pret. and pp. The more correct forms, rāht(e) and tāht(e), occur occasionally in both EWS and LWS.

INFLECTION: CONJUGATION. lxxvii

NOTE 5. — In LWS metathesis occasionally takes place in the pret. and pp. of **wyrc(e)an**: **wrohte, wroht**; and **forwyrhte, forwyrht** (with the vowel of the present) occur.

NOTE 6. — Occasionally in EWS and almost always in LWS the **ea** before **ht** in the pret. and pp. of verbs in **c** becomes **ę**; this is either by transference of the vowel of the present, or (less probably) by palatal-umlaut (**15**, Note 1): **cwęhte, (ge)cwęht; dręhte, (ge)dręht**, etc.

THE SECOND CLASS OF WEAK VERBS. (S. §§ 411-414.)

99. The class-suffix of verbs of the Second Conjugation is **-ō** (**94**); by the addition of **-jan** the full (infinitive) ending became *-ōjan, which by umlaut would become *-ējan, then by contraction -īan and finally -ian. Because of the original ō, the class-suffix in the form of **i** does not occasion umlaut or any other change that might be wrought by an original **i**; on the other hand the **-o** of the preterit and past participle may cause **u-o-a-umlaut** (**14**): **cliopode, cliopade** (**clipian**, *to cry out*): **hlinode, hlionode** (**hlinian**, *to lean*) etc.; and occasionally this umlaut is spread to the present so that forms like **cleopian (cliopian), hleonian (hlionian)** occur.

NOTE 1. — Umlaut appearing in a verb of this class is due either to transference from the First Class (**96**, 4 ; **97**, Note 4, *c*), or to the word from which the verb is derived : **ęndian**, *to end* [**ęnde**, *end*]; **clǣnsian**, *to cleanse* [**clǣne**, adj. jo-stem, *clean*].

CONJUGATION OF THE SECOND CLASS OF WEAK VERBS.

100. Themes: **bodian**, *to proclaim;* **smēag(e)an**, *to consider*.

PRESENT.

Indicative

Sing. 1.	bodie, (-ige)	smēage
2.	bodast	smēast
3.	bodaþ	smēaþ
Plur. 1–3.	bodiaþ, (-ig(e)aþ)	smēag(e)aþ

lxxviii *AN OUTLINE OF ANGLO-SAXON GRAMMAR.*

Optative.

Sing. 1–3.	bodie, (-ige)	smēage
Plur. 1–3.	bodien, (-igen)	smēagen

Imperative.

Sing. 2.	boda	smēa
Plur. 2.	bodiaðˇ, (-ig(e)aðˇ)	smēag(e)aðˇ

Infinitive.	bodian, (-ig(e)an)	smēag(e)an, (smēan)
Gerund.	{ bodianne, (-ig(e)anne, -enne, -onne)	smēag(e)anne
Pres. Part.	bodiende, (-igende)	smēagende

PRETERIT.

Indicative.

Sing. 1.	bodode, (-ade, -ude)	smēade
2.	bododest	smēadest
3.	bodode	smēade
Plur. 1–3.	bododon, (-edon)	smēadon

Optative.

Sing. 1–3.	bodode, (-ade, -ude)	smēade
Plur. 1–3.	bododen (-edon)	smēaden
Past Part.	(ge)bodod, (-ad, -ud)	(ge)smēad

NOTE 1. — In these verbs the graphic substitutions for ie, ia are common (11, Note 3).

NOTE 2. — The variant forms of the class-vowel o of the pret. are a, u; less frequently e, except in the pl., where e shares the preference equally with o.

NOTE 3. — trūwian, *to trust* (originally of the Third Class), and ðˇēowian, *to serve*, sometimes syncopate the middle vowel in the preterit: trūwde, ðˇēowde; with loss of the w, ðˇēode (ðˇēodde).

101. smēag(e)an (< *smēahōjan < *smauhōjan) represents a small number of contract verbs: fēog(e)an (< *fiōjan), *to hate;* frēog(e)an (< *friōjan), *to love,*

INFLECTION: CONJUGATION.   lxxix

to free; scōg(e)an (< *scōhōjan), *to shoe;* twēog(e)an (< *twehōjan), *to doubt;* ðrēag(e)an, *to rebuke;* *tēog(e)an (pret. tēode), *to arrange;* and apparently bōg(e)an (3 sg. bōð), *to boast.*

THE THIRD CLASS OF WEAK VERBS.   (S. §§ 415, 416.)

102. Weak verbs of the Third Class, of which the original class-suffix was -ai (**94**), are few in number, and these retain only in part the features of the original conjugation.

CONJUGATION OF THE THIRD CLASS OF WEAK VERBS.

103. Themes: **habban,** *to have;* **libban,** *to live;* sęcg(e)an, *to say.*

PRESENT.

Indicative.

Sing. 1.	hæbbe	libbe, lifge
2.	hafast, hæfst	liofast (14), lifast
3.	hafað, hæfð	liofað, lifað
Plur. 1-3.	habbað, hæbbað	libbað, lif(i)g(e)að, lifiað

Optative.

Sing. 1-3.	hæbbe	libbe, lifi(g)e
Plur. 1-3.	hæbben	libben, lifi(g)en

Imperative.

Sing. 2.	hafa	liofa
Plur. 2.	habbað	libbað, lif(i)g(e)að
Infinitive.	habban	{ libban, lif(i)g(e)an, lifian, lifian
Gerund.	habbanne, (-enne, -onne)	libbanne, lif(i)(g)enne
Pres. Part.	hæbbende	libbende, lif(i)(g)ende

PRETERIT.

Indicative.

Sing. 1.	hæfde	lifde, liofode
2.	hæfdest	lifdest, liofodest
3.	hæfde	lifde, liofode
Plur. 1–3.	hæfdon	lifdon, liofdon

Optative.

Sing. 1–3.	hæfde	lifde, liofode
Plur. 1–3.	hæfden	lifden, liofoden

Past Part. (ge)hæfd   (ge)lifd, (ge)liofod

NOTE. — **habban** with the negative adverb **ne** prefixed becomes **næbban**.

	PRESENT.	PRETERIT.
	Indicative.	
Sing. 1.	secge	sægde, sæde (16)
2.	sagast, sægst, segst	sægdest, sædest
3.	sagað, sæg(e)ð, seg(e)ð	sægde, sæde
Plur. 1–3.	secg(e)að	sægdon, sædon

Optative.

Sing. 1–3.	secge	sægde, sæde
Plur. 1–3.	secgen	sægden, sæden

Imperative.

Sing. 2.	saga, sege
Plur. 2.	secg(e)að

Infinitive.	secg(e)an	*Past Part.*	(ge)sægd, (ge)sæd
Gerund.	{ secg(e)anne, (-onne, secgenne) }		
Pres. Part.	secgende		

104. Traces of this conjugation are left in **fylg(e)an**, *to follow*, pret. **fylgde**, and **hycg(e)an**, *to think*, pret. **hogde**; but these verbs have besides conformed completely to the Second Conjugation: **folgian**, **folgode**; **hogian**, **hogode**.

INFLECTION: CONJUGATION. lxxxi

PRETERITIVE PRESENT VERBS. (S. §§ 417-425.)

105. (1) There are some verbs which, in all the Germanic languages, employ in the present exclusively (Indicative and Optative) forms of original ablaut preterits (the original presents being lost). Accordingly they are called preteritive present verbs.

The other parts of the system of present forms, namely, the Imperative, the Infinitive, the Gerund, and the Present Participle, are based upon the indicative plural of these preteritive presents. Upon the basis of the same form of the radical syllable, the conjugation of the tenses is made complete by weak preterits in **d (t)**; whereas the Past Participles (so far as they occur) like those of Strong verbs end in **-en**.

(2) These verbs are special in retaining some features of the more primitive conjugation of ablaut verbs: (*a*) the 2 sg. of the preteritive present is in **t** or **st**, without change of the radical syllable (cf. 93, Note); (*b*) there is a partial survival of the umlauted optative: **dyge, duge; ðyrfe, ðurfe.** On the other hand, the influence of the regular conjugation has occasioned such forms as pl. **(ge)munað**; 2 pl. imperative **witað**.

106. The preteritive present verbs are classified in accordance with their relation to the ablaut verbs:

(1) Class I.—(*a*) *Infinitive*, **witan (wietan; wiotan, weotan; 14).** *to know.*

	PRESENT.	PRETERIT.
Indicative sg. 1.	wāt	wi(e)ste, wisse
2.	wāst	
3.	wāt	wi(e)ste, wisse
pl. 1–3.	wi(e)ton, wioton (14)	wi(e)ston, wisson

	PRESENT.	PRETERIT.
Optative sg.	wi(e)te; pl. -en	wi(e)ste, wisse; pl. -en
Imperative sg. 2.	wite	*Past Part.* wi(e)ten
pl. 2.	witaðˇ	
Gerund.	wi(e)tanne, wiotonne. (-enne, etc.)	
Pres. Part.	witende	

NOTE 1.—nytan (< ne + witan), *not to know*, pres. indic. sg. nāt, nāst, nāt, pl. nyton, has uniformly y, for i (ie, io, eo), in the radical syllable.

(b) *Infinitive*, **āgan**, *to possess*.

Pres. Part., **āgende**.
Indicative., pres., sg. 1. 3. **āh (āg)**, 2. **āhst**; pl. **āgon**.
Optative, pres., **āge**, etc.   *Imperative*, **āge**.
Preterit, **āhte**, etc.   *Past Part.*, adj., **āgen, ǣgen**, *own*.

NOTE 2.—In the present the radical vowel of the singular has been transferred to the plural (āgon, for *igon), hence the uniformity of the radical vowel (infinitive āgan, pret. āhte, etc.). The negative theme is **nāgan** (< ne ÷ āgan), *not to possess*.

(2) Class II.—*Infinitive*, **dugan**, *to avail*.

Pres. Part., **dugende**.
Indicative, pres., sg. 1. 3. **dēah (dēag)**; pl. **dugon**.
Optative, pres., **dyge (105, 2), duge**, etc.
Preterit, **dohte**, etc.

(3) Class III.—(a) *Infinitive*, **unnan**, *to grant*.

Pres. Part., **unnende**.
Indicative, pres., sg. 1. 3. **ǫn(n), an(n)**; pl. **unnon**.
Optative, pres., **unne**, etc.   *Imperative*, **unne**.
Preterit, **ūðe**, etc.   *Past Part.*, **unnen**

INFLECTION: CONJUGATION. lxxxiii

(*b*) *Infinitive,* **cunnan,** *to know, can.*

Indicative, pres., sg. 1. 3. cǫn(n), can(n), 2. cǫnst; pl. cuunon.
Optative, pres., **cunne,** etc.
Preterit, **cūðe,** etc.   *Past Part.*. **cunnen**; adj., **cūð,** *known.*

(*c*) *Infinitive,* **ðurfan,** *to need.*

Pres. Part., **ðearfende.**
Indicative, pres., sg. 1. 3. **ðearf,** 2. **ðearft;** pl. **ðurfon.**
Optative, pres., **ðyrfe (105, 2), ðurfe,** etc.
Preterit, **ðorfte,** etc.

(*d*) *Infinitive,* **durran,** *to dare.*

Indicative, pres., sg. 1. 3. **dear(r),** 2. **dearst;** pl. **durron.**
Optative, pres., **dyrre (105, 2), durre,** etc.
Preterit, **dorste,** etc.

(4) Class IV. — (*a*) *Infinitive,* **sculan, sceolan,** *shall.*

Indicative, pres., sg. 1. 3. **sceal,** 2. **scealt;** pl. **sculon, sceolon.**
Optative, pres., **scyle, sci(e)le (105, 2), scule, sceole,** etc.
Preterit, **sceolde, scolde,** etc.

(*b*) *Infinitive,* **munan,** *to be mindful of.*

Pres. Part., **munende.**
Indicative, pres., sg. 1. 3. **mǫn, man,** 2. **mǫnst;** { pl. **munon, munað.**
Optative, pres., **myne (105, 2), mune,** etc.
Imperative, **myn(e), mun(e);** pl. **munað.**
Preterit, **munde,** etc.   *Past Part.,* **munen.**

(5) Class V. — (*a*) *Infinitive,* **magan,** *may, to be able.*

Indicative, pres., sg. 1. 3. **mæg,** 2. **meaht, miht;** { pl. **magon, mægon.**
Optative, pres., **mæge, mage,** etc.
Preterit, **meahte (mæhte, mehte), mihte,** etc.

lxxxiv *AN OUTLINE OF ANGLO-SAXON GRAMMAR.*

(b) *Infinitive*, (ge-, be-)**nugan**, *to suffice.*
   Indicative, pres., sg. 3. **neah** (impersonal); pl. **nugon**.
   Optative, pres., **nuge**, etc.
   Preterit, **nohte**, etc.

(6) Class VI. — *Infinitive*, **mōtan**, *may.*
   Indicative, pres., sg. 1. 3. **mōt**, 2. **mōst**; pl. **mōton**.
   Optative, pres., **mōte**, etc.
   Preterit, **mōste**, etc.

CONJUGATION OF SPECIAL VERBS.   (S. §§ 426–430.)

107. Several commonly used verbs in Anglo-Saxon represent pre-Germanic types or are so irregular that classification is useless. Note, however, that **wesan** is a regular fifth class strong verb, included here merely because it is used to supplement **bēon**.

Themes: (1) **bēon** (**wesan**), *to be;* (2) **willan**, *to will;* **dōn**, *to do;* (4) **gān**, *to go.*

(1)   PRESENT.   PRETERIT.
                        Indicative.

Sing. 1.   eom   bēom (bīom) bēo (bīo)   wæs
      2.   eart   bist   wǣre
      3.   is   bið   wæs
Plur. 1–3. { sind, si(e)nt
            si(e)ndon, -un bēoð (bīoð)   wǣron
            siondon, -un

                        Optative.

Sing. 1–3. sie (sī, sig, sȳ), sīo (sēo)   bēo (bīo)   wǣre
Plur. 1–3. sīen (sīn, sȳn)   bēon (bīon) wǣren

Imperative. 2 sg. bēo, wes; 2 pl. bēoð, wesað
Infinitive. bēon (bīon), wesan
Gerund.   bēonne (bīonne)
Pres. Part. bēonde, wesende

NOTE 1. — Negative forms are neom (<**ne** + **eom**), nis (<**ne** + **is**); næs (<**ne** + **wæs**), nǣre, nǣron, etc.

INFLECTION: CONJUGATION.

Note 2. — Some of the special features of this verb are : (*a*) the employment of different roots ; (*b*) traces of non-thematic conjugation, such as m for the ending of the 1 sg. pres. indic. (**eom, bēom**); (*c*) the ending -**on** (-**un**) of the pres. indic. pl. (**sindon**, etc.), which is due to the influence of the preteritive presents.

(2)   Present.   Preterit.

Indicative.

Sing. 1.	wille (wielle), wile	wolde
2.	wilt	woldest
3.	wille (wielle), wile	wolde
Plur. 1–3.	willaÞ (wiellaÞ)	woldon

Optative.

Sing. 1–3.	wille (wielle), wile	wolde
Plur. 1–3.	willen (wiellen)	wolden

Imperative. (only with negative) 2 pl. **nyllaÞ, nellaÞ**
Infinitive.   willan (wiellan)
Pres. Part. willende (wiellende)

Note 3. — The negative **nyllan** (< ne + willan), pret. **nolde**, etc., has usually the vowel **y** or **e** in the radical syllable of the present: **nylle, nelle**, etc.

Note 4. — **willan** is special in having derived its Present Indicative from the Optative. The 2 sg. **wilt** is in conformity with the preteritive presents, and the pl. **willaÞ** is the result of the influence of the regular conjugation.

(3)   Present.   Preterit.

Indicative.

Sing. 1.	dō	dyde
2.	dēst	dydest
3.	dēÞ	dyde
Plur. 1–3.	dōÞ	dydon

Optative.

Sing. 1–3.	dō	dyde
Plur. 1–3.	dōn	dyden

Imperative. 2 sg. dō ; 2 pl. dōÞ   *Past Part.* { dōn / dēn
Infinitive.   dōn   *Gerund.*   dōnne
Pres. Part. dōnde (dōende)

NOTE 5. — **dōn** is a non-thematic verb (dialectal 1 sg. pres. indic. **dōm**), and has as preterit a form not satisfactorily explained.

(4)   PRESENT.   PRETERIT.
                            Indicative.
   Sing. 1.   **gā**   **ēode**
        2.   **gǣst**   **ēodest**
        3.   **gǣð**   **ēode**
   Plur. 1–3. **gāð**   **ēodon**
                            Optative.
   Sing. 1–3. **gā**   **ēode**
   Plur. 1–3. **gān**   **ēoden**

   Imperative. 2 sg. **gā**; 2 pl. **gāð**   *Past Part.* **gān**
   Infinitive. **gān**
   Gerund.   **gānne**
   Pres. Part. **gānde**

NOTE 6. — The non-thematic verb **gān** has a special feature in the preterit **ēode**, which in use is also associated with the present **gọngan** (**90**, Note 3).

For Product Safety Concerns and Information please contact our EU representative GPSR@taylorandfrancis.com
Taylor & Francis Verlag GmbH, Kaufingerstraße 24, 80331 München, Germany

www.ingramcontent.com/pod-product-compliance
Lightning Source LLC
Chambersburg PA
CBHW052135300426
44116CB00010B/1909